THE EMOTIONAL INTELLIGENCE AND RESILIENCE HANDBOOK

The Emotional Intelligence and Resilience Handbook

Practical Tools for Growth, Connection, and Leadership for Everyone

SHIRITA NASH

ACC, ODCP, SHRM-CP

ISBN: 979-8-9923521-0-8

Book Design by Christian Storm

To my mother, Faye, the cornerstone of my strength and resilience. Your unwavering love, endless sacrifices, and tireless belief in me have shaped the person I am today. You've taught me the value of perseverance, the power of empathy, and the importance of staying true to myself, no matter the challenges. This book is a testament to the lessons you've instilled in me and the foundation you've built for my success. I am forever grateful for your guidance, your wisdom, and your unshakable faith in my journey.

This is for you, with all my love.

Contents

Acknowledgments

Writing this book has been a journey of reflection, growth, and gratitude. It is not just the culmination of my experiences and insights but also a testament to the incredible people who have shaped, supported, and inspired me along the way.

To my husband, Terdell, your unwavering love and belief in me have been the foundation of everything I do. Thank you for being my partner, my cheerleader, and my rock.

To my children, Olivia and Tyson, you are my heart and my greatest inspiration. Watching you grow and thrive fuels my passion for leaving a meaningful legacy.

To my mother, Faye, father, John, and stepmother, Novlette, your guidance and support have been the anchors in my life. Thank you for instilling in me the values of perseverance and compassion.

To my siblings—Reshell, John, Darwin, Travis, and Nakia—thank you for your love, encouragement, and laughter. You remind me of the importance of family and the strength we draw from one another.

To my sorority line sisters—Tiffany, Ronda, Dorothy, Kaneesha, Nadege, Sutanne, Kiana, and Nicole—and my Delta Sigma Theta Sorority sisters, your sisterhood and shared purpose have enriched my life in countless ways. Thank you for always uplifting and inspiring me.

To my colleagues at the National Aeronautics and Space Administration (NASA), your dedication and excellence have been a source of motivation and pride. It is an honor to work alongside such brilliant minds.

To my friends and extended family, your love and encouragement have been a constant source of strength. Thank you for walking this journey with me.

To George Mason University, the University of South Florida, and Nova Southeastern University, thank you for providing the educational foundations that have shaped my career and personal growth.

To my mentors and supervisors throughout my journey, your wisdom and guidance have left an indelible mark on my life. Thank you for believing in me and pushing me to reach my full potential.

To my clients, thank you for trusting me to be part of your journey. Your courage, vulnerability, and commitment to growth have inspired me more than you could ever know. Working with you has not only shaped this book but has also deepened my understanding of the transformative power of emotional intelligence and resilience.

To the countless authors, coaches, and thought leaders whose insights and writings have informed my understanding of these topics. This book is a reflection of the many ways you have all contributed to my story. I am endlessly grateful for your presence in my life and the role you've played in helping me bring this vision to life.

With deepest gratitude,

Coach Shirita Nash

THE EMOTIONAL INTELLIGENCE AND RESILIENCE HANDBOOK

Introduction

A Song Worth Singing

Joan Walsh Anglund once wrote, "A bird does not sing because it has an answer, it sings because it has a song." This quote embodies the heart of why I decided to publish my first book. For years, I felt like the bird—knowing I had a voice, but waiting, listening, wondering if the time was right to share my song.

I could always sing. But I wanted to ensure that when I did, my song would carry meaning—a melody of beauty, resilience, and wisdom that might inspire others. A melody that would add life to others and harmonize with the world around me. I didn't want to speak just to fill the silence; I wanted to offer something that resonates, something that matters.

This book is my song. It grew from years of personal experiences that shaped me: the moments that tested my strength, the connections that brought me joy, and the lessons I gained through navigating life's challenges. As a coach, a professional, a mother, and a fellow human, I've seen the profound impact of emotional intelligence and resilience—not just in myself, but in others. This book became the natural expression of my desire to share those lessons, to give others the tools to thrive in their own lives.

To sing is an act of courage, and this book is my act of courage. It's my way of saying, "Here is what I've learned; here is what has helped me grow and connect with others." My hope is that my stories, insights, and tools will resonate with you and help you find and sing your own song—a song of growth, connection, and transformation.

I don't have all the answers, but I have this song. And I am so grateful for the chance to share it with you.

Introduction to the Author

As a certified coach, organizational development professional, and lifelong advocate for personal growth, I have dedicated my career to uncovering and understanding the powerful connections between emotional intelligence, resilience, and effective leadership. My journey encompasses a rich tapestry of academic accomplishments, numerous certifications, expertise in facilitating inventory assessments, professional experience in human resources, and countless hours devoted to guiding individuals and teams through challenges and toward achieving their goals. The motivation to write this book stems from witnessing the transformative power of emotional intelligence and resilience in action—not only in my own life but also in the lives of those I've had the privilege to coach. I have always wanted to help people, and this book gives me the opportunity to expand my reach, sharing these insights with a wider audience. With a passion for helping people think, evaluate, and act with clarity and purpose, I knew it was time to bring these tools and stories to life in a way that could make a meaningful difference.

This Book's Purpose

This book is designed to be more than just a guide—it's a playbook for anyone seeking to enhance their emotional intelligence and strengthen their resilience. Through its chapters, you'll find tools, stories, and reflections that address the complexities of modern life. Whether you're navigating personal transitions, leading teams, or building relationships, this book offers actionable strategies to foster growth and connection. In a world where change and uncertainty are constants, developing these skills has never been more important. My hope is that this book will equip readers with the insights and confidence to embrace challenges and thrive.

Why This Book is Unique

This book stands out because of its blend of deeply personal stories, practical coaching activities, and research-based insights. Each chapter begins with an original quote that sets the tone and ends with a hands-on exercise or worksheet to encourage reflection and action. By weaving together theory and practice, the material bridges the gap between understanding and application. It's not just about learning concepts—it's about living them. The integration of metaphors and coaching techniques creates a resource that resonates on multiple levels for a unique and enriching read.

Audience Connection

This book is for anyone ready to grow—whether you're a leader guiding a team, a professional navigating change, a spouse working on empathy, a student pursuing knowledge and self-awareness, or an individual striving for personal development. If you've ever felt stuck, unsure, or overwhelmed, this book offers clarity and direction. It's written with you in mind, recognizing the challenges you face and providing tools to help you move forward. No matter where you are in your journey, the strategies in this book will meet you there and support your next steps.

How to Use This Book

This book is your guide to building emotional intelligence and resilience through practical strategies and meaningful insights. It's broken down into 10 specific topics that serve as the foundation for growth in these critical areas. Whether you choose to read it cover to cover or skip to chapters that address your immediate needs, it's designed to meet you where you are and support your unique journey.

1. Flexible Structure: Guide Your Own Path

Each chapter is self-contained, allowing you to dive into the topics that resonate most with you in the moment. Whether you're facing a personal challenge, navigating a professional hurdle, or simply seeking inspiration, you can select the chapters that fill the gaps you need to address. Alternatively, reading the book sequentially provides a comprehensive roadmap to leaning into emotional intelligence and resilience.

2. Reflection Questions: Contemplate the Why and How

At the end of each chapter, you'll find a series of reflection questions. These are thoughtfully crafted to cultivate self-awareness, encourage meaningful reflection, and help you pause, delve deeper, and connect the concepts directly to your own experiences. Taking the time to answer these questions will allow you to uncover insights about your strengths, areas for growth, and opportunities for action. Write your responses in a journal or notebook and revisit them periodically to track your progress and evolving perspectives.

3. Practical Activities: Discover the Why and How

Following the reflection questions, each chapter includes a hands-on activity or coaching exercise. These activities are the bridge between understanding and action, helping you apply what you've learned in a tangible, practical way. Whether it's a personal exercise or a team-building activity, these tools are designed to deepen your learning and help you see real results. Approach these activities with an open mind and adapt them as needed to fit your specific context.

4. Reusable Material: Revisit and Reapply

Growth isn't a one-time event—it's a lifelong process. Use this book as a resource you can return to whenever you face new challenges or want to deepen your understanding. The reflection questions and activities can offer new insights and solutions as you grow and evolve.

5. Interactive Opportunities: Share and Collaborate

This book is also a tool for connection. Share the activities with your team, friends, colleagues, spouse, organization, or church. Use the questions to ignite meaningful conversations or explore the concepts further with a coach or mentor. By applying these strategies in your interactions with others, you can create a ripple effect of growth and resilience. You can reach out to me at www.AcnestisCG.com and https://www.linkedin.com/in/shiritanash/. If this book resonates with you, I would love to hear your thoughts or feedback.

Whether you're making small strides or taking bold leaps, this book is here to support and guide you. Approach each chapter with purpose, engage with the reflection questions thoughtfully, and embrace the activities as opportunities for meaningful growth. Together, these tools will empower you to cultivate the emotional intelligence and resilience needed to flourish in every area of your life. Let this book be your trusted playbook for personal and professional success.

Chapter 1

The Foundations of Emotional Intelligence

- DEFINING EMOTIONAL INTELLIGENCE
- REFLECTION: BUILDING YOUR EMOTIONAL INTELLIGENCE
- ACTIVITY: EMOTIONAL INTELLIGENCE WHEEL

I

The Foundations of Emotional Intelligence

"Now you know, and knowing is half the battle."
—G.I. Joe

Imagine this: You're circling a crowded parking lot, already running late, your patience thinning with every lap. Finally, you spot it—a perfect spot just a few feet away. You turn on your blinker, ready to pull in, but out of nowhere, another car swoops in and takes it. To top it off, the driver steps out, looks at you, and smiles as if they've done you a favor. Your frustration boils over, and you're tempted to roll down your window and let them know exactly how you feel. But then you pause, grip the steering wheel tighter, and realize this is the kind of situation that ends up on someone's viral TikTok feed titled, "Parking Lot Meltdown." So, instead, you take a deep breath, drive off to find another spot, and mutter something under your breath that you would never hear on the Disney channel. Beep. Beep. Beep. Sound familiar?

When moments like these happen—and they will—it's easy to let emotions take the wheel, driving our actions before we even realize it. But it's in these small, everyday challenges that self-awareness steps in. It's that moment when we recognize our own emotions and understand how they shape our thoughts and influence our choices. This is where emotional intelligence begins—not just in keeping calm, but in pausing to reflect and using that knowledge to respond intentionally. And while self-awareness is a critical step, it's only half the battle.

Self-awareness is the foundation of emotional intelligence, much like the base of a house. It provides the stability and direction needed to build something greater, but the rest of the structure depends on other essential skills: self-regulation, empathy, social skills, and motivation. Together, these elements complete the framework, helping us navigate life's challenges with clarity, resilience, and purpose. Knowing yourself gives you the foundation, but it's what you do with that knowledge that makes all the difference.

Sometimes, though, self-awareness feels less like a foundation and more like a bright light shining on things we'd rather keep in the shadows. It can be uncomfortable, even humbling, but it's also where real growth begins. Recognizing our emotions and patterns gives us the power to make better choices—to respond thoughtfully instead of reacting impulsively, and to turn misunderstandings into opportunities for connection.

One experience in particular taught me this lesson in a way I'll never forget. It was a seemingly ordinary day in the office, but a brief email changed everything. What could have spiraled into frustration and conflict became a moment of connection—because I chose to pause, reflect, and lead with curiosity instead of defensiveness. Let me take you back to that day.

Turning a Misunderstanding into a Connection

It was a busy afternoon in the office, and I was immersed in an employee relations investigation. These cases were always high-stakes, requiring meticulous attention to detail, discretion, and thoughtful communication. I had just received an email from a colleague assisting with the investigation. The email was brief and direct, but the tone felt curt, almost dismissive. Worse, it seemed to imply that I hadn't handled certain steps of the investigation properly.

Immediately, I felt a surge of defensiveness. I had poured hours into carefully reviewing policies, interviewing involved parties, and documenting every step. My mind raced with justifications and counterpoints. As frustration grew, I started typing a reply, outlining the thoroughness of my work and subtly pointing out areas where her contributions had fallen short. My emotions were fueling the response, and I could feel the tension in my typing.

But just as I was about to hit "Send," I paused. Something didn't feel right. I took a deep breath and asked myself: "What's really happening here? Could there be more to this than I'm assuming?" It struck me that I might be projecting my own stress onto her words. After all, employee relations investigations are inherently stressful, not just for HR but for everyone involved. Could it be that her tone reflected the pressure she was under, rather than a criticism of my efforts?

Instead of sending the email, I decided to give her a call. Picking up the phone felt like a small but meaningful shift. When she answered, I opened the conversation with care: "Hey, I got your email, and I wanted to check in. It sounds like you might have some concerns about the process—can we talk about it?"

Her response caught me off guard. I could hear the exhaustion in her voice as she said, "I'm so sorry if my email came off as harsh. I've been juggling multiple cases this week, and I'm just trying to make sure nothing gets missed in this one. I didn't mean to sound critical."

In that moment, everything clicked. Her email wasn't about me—it was about the stress she was carrying. By choosing to pause and approach her with empathy instead of defensiveness, I had defused what could have become a tense, unproductive conflict. Not only did we resolve the immediate misunderstanding, but we also strengthened our working relationship. The collaboration that followed was smoother, more open, and far more effective.

Reflecting on this experience later, I realized how easily it could have gone differently. Had I sent that defensive email, I might have escalated tensions and damaged our professional rapport. Instead, I chose to pause, regulate my emotions, and assume positive intent. That decision taught me an invaluable lesson: In moments of tension, it's often our ability to pause and approach others with curiosity and compassion that makes the greatest difference.

This experience didn't just change how I approached investigations in HR—it fundamentally shifted how I handled difficult conversations in both life and business. Whether working on sensitive employee issues, navigating workplace challenges, or addressing personal conflicts, I learned the transformative power of leading with empathy and seeking clarity before reacting. These skills became essential in fostering trust, resolving misunderstandings, and turning emotionally charged situations into opportunities for growth and connection. It was a defining moment in my journey toward understanding emotional intelligence, reminding me that navigating emotions—both my own and those of others—is not just about reacting in the moment but about pausing, reflecting, and approaching challenges with intention and empathy.

These skills, however, don't develop by chance. They are part of a larger framework that shapes how we understand ourselves, interact with others, and make decisions. Emotional intelligence is the foundation of this framework—a dynamic, multifaceted skill set that extends beyond self-awareness to include self-regulation, empathy, social skills, and intrinsic motivation. Let's dive deeper into these essential components and explore how they contribute to personal growth and meaningful connections.

Defining Emotional Intelligence

Emotional intelligence is the ability to recognize, understand, and manage our own emotions while effectively perceiving and influencing the emotions of others (Goleman, 1995)—and not just crying during a rom-com or being the office cheerleader. It's a finely-tuned superpower, minus the cape, that fuels personal growth and professional success. It is a skill that goes beyond IQ, shaping how we navigate relationships, respond to challenges, and lead fulfilling lives.

At its core, emotional intelligence is built on several interconnected components that work together to help us understand ourselves and interact meaningfully with others.

Let's take a closer look at each of these essential elements:

1. Self-Awareness:

Often regarded as the cornerstone of emotional intelligence, self-awareness is the ability to accurately recognize and understand your own feelings and emotions, as well as their impact on your thoughts, behaviors, and decisions (Goleman, 1995). Self-awareness isn't just about identifying feelings—it's about digging deeper to understand why you feel a certain way and how those emotions influence your interactions. Building self-awareness is like being your own detective—uncovering your values, strengths, and those pesky areas where you still have room to grow (we all have them, don't worry!).

For instance, imagine you're feeling irritated during a team meeting. Instead of lashing out or shutting down, you pause to reflect on what's causing your frustration. You realize it's not the team's suggestions but rather the stress from an earlier deadline. With this awareness, you can prevent your emotions from affecting the discussion and focus on solutions.

2. Self-Regulation:

Life is full of unexpected challenges, and how we respond to those moments can define our trajectory. Self-regulation is the ability to self-manage and control your emotional reactions, particularly in high-stress or unpredictable situations (Bradberry & Greaves, 2009). It's what allows you to pause before reacting, to redirect anger into constructive communication, or to stay calm under pressure when others may lose focus. Self-regulation isn't about bottling up your emotions like a shaken soda can; it's about turning that fizz into fuel for something productive (and less messy).

For instance, imagine receiving negative feedback on a project you worked hard on. Instead of reacting defensively or becoming discouraged, you take a deep breath, thank the person for their input, and take time to process it. Later, you review the feedback objectively and make a plan to improve, turning a potentially upsetting moment into a growth opportunity.

3. Empathy:

Empathy is often described as the heart of emotional intelligence, and for good reason. It's the ability to truly understand and connect with another person's feelings and perspective (Goleman, 1995). Empathy isn't about being a superhero swooping in to solve everyone's problems or nodding like a bobblehead at everything they say; it's about creating a space where people feel truly seen, heard, and valued—cape optional.

For instance, imagine a colleague who seems distracted and withdrawn during a meeting. Instead of assuming they're uninterested or unprofessional, you take the time to ask how they're doing. They share that they're dealing with a family issue, and you offer support or flexibility. That moment of empathy strengthens trust and opens the door for better collaboration.

4. Social Skills:

Emotional intelligence shines most brightly in our relationships with others. Social skills are the tools that enable us to manage and maintain relationships, navigate complex social dynamics, and communicate effectively (Bradberry & Greaves, 2009). Strong social skills include active listening, effective verbal and nonverbal communication, conflict resolution, and the ability to inspire and influence others. Think of it as having the ultimate people skills toolkit—perfect for everything from diffusing office drama to winning over your in-laws.

For instance, imagine a team brainstorming session where tensions rise as people talk over one another. Instead of letting the chaos continue, you step in to facilitate. You summarize each person's ideas, ensure everyone has a chance to speak, and guide the discussion back on track. Your ability to manage the group dynamics fosters a productive and respectful environment.

5. Motivation:

Finally, emotional intelligence includes an intrinsic motivation that drives us to pursue goals and fulfillment with passion (Goleman,

1995). Unlike external motivators, such as rewards or recognition, intrinsic motivation is fueled by our internal desire for growth, achievement, and purpose. It helps us maintain optimism and resilience, even in the face of setbacks— because when life throws you lemons, sometimes the best thing you can do is throw them back, showing life you're not easily shaken, and then build something even greater, like a full-on lemonade stand!

For instance, imagine working on a long-term project at work where success isn't guaranteed, and the immediate rewards are minimal. While others may lose interest or feel discouraged, intrinsic motivation keeps you going because you're driven by the satisfaction of mastering a new skill, solving a challenging problem, or contributing to something meaningful. It's the inner voice that reminds you why you started in the first place and keeps you focused on the bigger picture.

Together, these components form a powerful framework for understanding ourselves and navigating relationships with clarity, compassion, and purpose. Emotional intelligence is not a fixed trait—it is a skill that can be cultivated and strengthened over time. As we explore emotional intelligence in this chapter, I invite you to reflect on how these elements show up in your life. Consider the ways they influence your interactions, decisions, and personal growth—because developing emotional intelligence is not just about improving how we interact with others—it's about transforming our relationship with ourselves and the world around us.

The Mirror and the Compass

As we delve deeper, it's important to reflect on the dual role emotional intelligence plays in our lives. It's both a mirror and a compass. It serves as a mirror by allowing us to see ourselves clearly—our emotions, triggers, strengths, and areas for growth. Through self-awareness, we develop the ability to understand what drives our actions and how we influence those around us. But self-awareness is only the beginning. Emotional intelligence is also a compass, guiding us through relationships, decisions, and challenges. It shows us the way forward when emotions run high, helping us navigate conflicts, connect with others, and stay grounded in our values. Just as a hiker needs both tools to traverse unknown terrain, we need emotional intelligence to thrive in the complexities of life. The mirror keeps us honest about who we are, while the compass ensures we remain aligned with where we want to go.

With these tools in hand, we can transform our relationships, lead with empathy, and pursue our goals with resilience and clarity. As you continue this journey through the book, remember to check in with both the mirror and the compass. Each step forward begins with understanding yourself, but it's the guidance of emotional intelligence that will help you navigate toward growth and connection.

As we close this discussion, it's clear that emotional intelligence provides the mirror to understand ourselves and the compass to navigate our relationships and decisions. But knowing is only half the journey—application is where transformation happens. The components of emotional intelligence aren't just something to understand—they're skills that grow through intentional practice and self-reflection. This is your opportunity to think deeply about your emotions, evaluate your habits, and identify actionable steps.

In the next section, you'll have the opportunity to reflect on how emotional intelligence shows up in your life. Through guided questions, you'll explore your self-awareness, evaluate your emotional patterns, and identify actionable steps to strengthen your emotional intelligence. These exercises are designed to help you turn insights into meaningful progress, equipping you to face challenges with clarity, empathy, and resilience.

Reflection

Building Your Emotional Intelligence

Now that we've explored the foundations of emotional intelligence, let's take a moment to pause and reflect on how these concepts show up in your own life.

Grab a journal, a quiet space, and an open mind. As you answer the following questions, focus on being honest and curious with yourself. These prompts are designed to help you uncover patterns, clarify your values, and take meaningful steps toward growth. Let's begin this journey of self-discovery with your awareness of how emotions influence your decisions and relationships.

Think (Understanding & Awareness)

Consider these questions to explore your current understanding:

1. What does self-awareness mean to you in your daily life?
2. How do you think emotions influence your decision-making processes?
3. What emotions do you experience most often, and why?
4. How do your relationships reflect your level of emotional intelligence?
5. What role do your core values play in shaping your emotional reactions?

Evaluate (Analyzing & Reflecting)

Take time to analyze and reflect on your emotional habits and patterns:

1. How effectively do you regulate your emotions during stressful situations?
2. Reflect on a recent emotional reaction: What triggered it, and what was the outcome?
3. How do you currently balance emotional responses with rational thinking?
4. Which emotional intelligence skill (e.g., self-awareness, empathy, self-regulation) is your greatest strength?
5. In what areas of your life does emotional intelligence need improvement?

Act (Implementation & Practice)

Turn your reflections into action with these practical steps:

1. What small daily habit can you adopt to improve your self-awareness?
2. How can you actively practice empathy in one of your relationships this week?
3. What tools (journaling, mindfulness, feedback) will you use to track your emotional intelligence growth?
4. How can you create a support system to help you develop emotional intelligence skills?
5. What specific action will you take today to better manage your emotions in challenging situations?

As you work through these reflections and action steps, keep in mind that growth is a journey, not a destination. It takes patience, curiosity, and a willingness to embrace small, consistent changes. You don't need to have all the answers right away—what matters is your commitment to take that first step and keep moving forward.

To help you on this journey, we'll use the Emotional Intelligence Wheel as a tool for deeper exploration. This wheel provides a structured way to assess where you are now and identify areas for growth across the key components of emotional intelligence. By reflecting on each section, you'll gain clarity on your strengths, pinpoint areas for improvement, and create a focused plan for building emotional intelligence that aligns with your personal and professional goals.

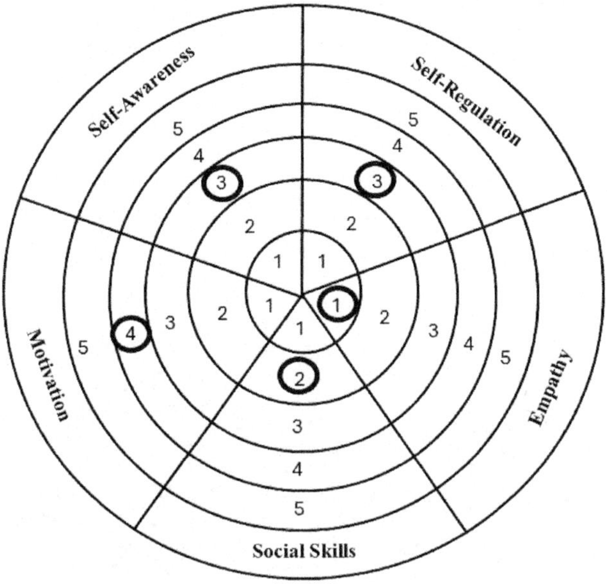

Activity

Wheel of Emotional Intelligence

This activity is designed to help you assess your current levels of emotional intelligence, reflect on your strengths and areas for improvement, and create a plan for growth. Please use this worksheet or your journal to guide your introspection.

Individual Wheel Assessment

Rate yourself on a scale of 1–5 by circling one number under each segment. A score of 1 indicates a lower level of satisfaction or effectiveness, and a score of 5 indicates a high level of satisfaction or effectiveness in that area.

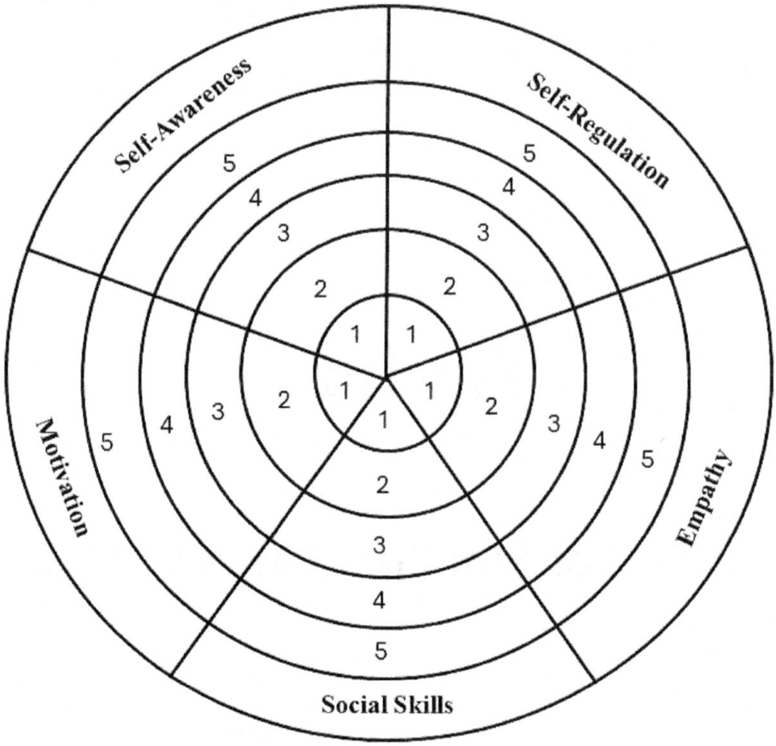

Initial Introspection

Reflect on your ratings and answer the following questions:

- What stands out to you as you look at your wheel?
- What areas of your wheel's score surprise you?
- What areas of the wheel do you feel most and least confident about?
- What patterns do you notice in your wheel?
- How do you feel about your overall level of emotional intelligence?

Identifying Areas for Improvement

Identify one area on your wheel where you would like to improve.

Action Planning

Develop one concrete action plan for improving the area identified above. To ensure your plan is effective, consider using the SMART framework. SMART goals are:

Specific: Clearly define what you want to achieve.
Measurable: Include criteria to track progress and know when the goal is accomplished.
Achievable: Ensure the goal is realistic and within your capabilities.
Relevant: Align the goal with your broader objectives or values.
Time-bound: Set a clear deadline or timeframe for completion.

For example:

Non-SMART goal: *"I want to improve my communication skills."*

SMART goal: *"I want to improve my communication skills. I will attend one communication workshop this month and practice active listening in two team meetings each week for the next three months."*

Another example:

Non-SMART goal: *"I need to be more organized."*

SMART goal: *"I want to be more organized. I will dedicate 15 minutes each evening to organizing my workspace and create a to-do list for the next day, starting this week."*

Using this framework ensures that your action plan is clear and actionable, giving you the best chance to succeed.

Now, revisit the area you identified above and create a SMART goal to guide your progress.

Reflection

Reflect on the activity and answer the following questions:

- What are your key takeaways from this activity?
- How will you apply these insights in your daily life?
- How do you think improving your emotional intelligence will impact your personal and professional life?

Next Steps

Revisit your wheel once every three months. During this time, check on your progress. Are your action plans working? What changes to the plan do you need to make? Do you need to continue working on this area or are you ready to focus on a new area of the wheel?

Closing the Chapter: The Foundations of Emotional Intelligence

In this chapter, we explored how emotional intelligence is both a mirror and a compass—a tool to reflect on who we are and a guide to navigate the complexities of life; learning how self-awareness serves as the foundation of emotional intelligence and the gateway to understanding our emotions, behaviors, and interactions.

But as we've seen, emotional intelligence extends beyond self-awareness to encompass the skills that help us build stronger connections, foster empathy, and approach challenges with clarity and resilience. After all, it's the magic trick that helps us keep our cool when life feels like a juggling act with one too many balls in the air.

As we move forward, we'll dive into the next crucial piece of this journey: resilience. Emotional intelligence equips us with the ability to understand and manage our emotions, but resilience allows us to bounce back from setbacks and navigate adversity with courage and determination. Together, these skills create a powerful framework for personal growth and success.

Take a moment to reflect on the lessons of this chapter. Think about how self-awareness and emotional intelligence have already shown up in your life and where you have opportunities to grow. With this foundation in place, let's turn to the next chapter to explore the art of resilience and how it can transform challenges into stepping stones for growth and strength.

Or, feel free to turn to the chapter that resonates most with where you are right now—the choice is yours to make this journey your own.

Chapter 2

Resilience—The Art of Bouncing Back

- DEFINING RESILIENCE
- REFLECTION: BUILDING YOUR RESILIENCE
- ACTIVITY: RESILIENCE RECIPE

2

Resilience—The Art of Bouncing Back

"I have made missteps along the way. But I have discovered the secret that after climbing a great hill, one only finds that there are many more hills to climb."

—Nelson Mandela

Have you ever faced a moment so challenging that you weren't sure how you'd make it through? Maybe it was the loss of someone you loved, the crushing blow of a dream deferred, or the overwhelming pressure of responsibilities piling up with no clear way out. A time when the weight of it all felt so heavy that getting out of bed, taking the next step, or even just breathing felt like monumental tasks. Inhale. Exhale.

I've been there. For me, that moment came with a loss so profound it tested every part of me—emotionally, mentally, and spiritually. The loss of my child was a climb I never expected, and it reshaped my understanding of what it means to endure and find strength.

Nelson Mandela's words remind us that life's challenges are not a single, insurmountable obstacle but a series of hills that test our resolve and shape our character. Each climb brings its own trials, but it also offers a moment to reflect, to gather strength, and to prepare for what lies ahead.

Resilience doesn't erase pain or hardship; instead, it gives us the capacity to endure, adapt, and grow through life's most difficult moments. It's the thread that connects the struggles we face to the strength we discover within ourselves. Like Mandela's metaphor, resilience teaches us that after every peak, there's another climb waiting—not to discourage us, but to remind us that we are capable of enduring and overcoming, again and again.

Let me take you into my story—a journey through grief, pain, and eventually, healing—where resilience became not just a concept, but a necessity.

Personal Resilience Story: Navigating the Loss of a Child During Pregnancy

When my husband and I decided to try for a third child, we were filled with excitement and hope. The news of my pregnancy brought joy to our home, and we immediately began planning for our growing family. We were thrilled about the chaos that would soon define our lives, knowing our kids would officially outnumber us. We brainstormed creative ways to share the news with our kids, like special "big brother" and "big sister" shirts and fortune cookies with messages revealing our family's newest addition. I bought maternity clothes and even a book for my son about becoming a big brother. Every step deepened our anticipation for this new chapter. This was everything we had hoped for. We were already deeply in love with the little one we hadn't yet met.

Then came the routine appointment—the one I assured my husband he didn't need to attend because it would be quick. "No, honey, you don't need to take off from work. I'll call you when I leave the doctor's office." I remember lying on the examination table as the doctor began the ultrasound. Something felt different. The room was too quiet, and the doctor's face didn't show the reassuring smile I was used to. After five minutes of silence, I finally asked, trying to ease the tension, "Is there a baby in there?" The doctor's response shattered my world: "I'm trying to find the heartbeat."

In that instant, my heart broke. No, it shattered! I couldn't breathe. The weight of those words crushed the joy and dreams we had already built for our family. I asked the doctor for a few minutes alone. Sitting in that room alone, I felt an overwhelming wave of grief and disbelief. The loss of our baby was more than the loss of a pregnancy; it was the loss of hope, plans, and the vision of our future.

Finding Resilience in the Midst of Grief

In the days that followed, I allowed myself to grieve. I cried when I needed to and leaned on my husband for support as we processed the loss together. But as the initial shock wore off, I realized I had a choice: I could either let the pain consume me or find a way to honor this experience and move forward with strength.

One of the most significant steps I took was starting therapy. I began seeing a therapist every week, and just talking became my therapy. Having a safe, judgment-free space to express my grief, anger, and confusion helped me process emotions I didn't even realize I was holding. I learned that it was okay to feel everything—heartache, frustration, even guilt—and that those feelings didn't define me or my ability to heal. I explored coping strategies that helped me understand

grief wasn't something to "get over," but something to live with in a way that honored my experience.

Talking through my emotions also gave me clarity. It helped me untangle the complex thoughts swirling in my mind and allowed me to find moments of peace amidst the storm. Each session felt like lifting a weight off my chest, reminding me that healing doesn't come all at once but in small, steady steps. Therapy became a crucial tool in my journey of resilience, giving me the emotional support and perspective I needed to move forward.

Another practice that became vital to my healing was gratitude journaling. I turned to journaling as another outlet for reflection and healing, helping me name the pain while also acknowledging moments of gratitude. At first, it felt impossible to think of anything I could be grateful for in the midst of such a profound loss. But as I began to write, small things emerged—moments of love from my family, the kindness of friends, the strength I didn't know I had. Gratitude journaling didn't erase the pain, but it shifted my perspective. It reminded me that even in heartbreak, life offered reasons to hope, things to be grateful for, and moments to cherish. Writing down these moments each day gave me a sense of grounding and helped me focus on the positives that still existed, even as I navigated the grief.

Gratitude journaling also became a way to honor my child's memory. Instead of fixating on what I had lost, I started to recognize the ways this experience had deepened my appreciation for the love and connections in my life. It gave me a tool to hold onto joy even on the hardest days and a pathway to heal without feeling like I was leaving the memory behind.

Seeking connection, I also leaned into my family for comfort, especially my children, who unknowingly became a source of resilience for me. Their laughter reminded me of the blessings I already had, even in the face of this heartbreaking loss. I opened up to close friends and family about the loss. To my surprise, many shared their own experiences with pregnancy loss—stories I had never known. Their courage and empathy helped me feel less isolated, reminding me that grief was something I didn't have to face alone.

How Resilience Made Me a Better Coach

My experience of learning resiliency not only shaped me personally but also transformed me professionally. As a coach, I now approach my clients with a deeper sense of empathy and understanding. Experiencing such profound grief taught me that everyone carries invisible burdens. It reminded me of the importance of creating a safe, judgment-free space for others—just as my therapist had done for me. I learned to listen more intentionally, to meet people where they are, and to guide them through their challenges with patience and compassion.

The tools I developed during my own healing journey—like gratitude journaling—became practical exercises I could offer to clients. I also became more attuned to helping clients process their emotions, move forward at their own pace, and find strength within themselves.

Resilience gave me the ability to connect with others on a deeper level. It taught me that growth often comes from the hardest experiences and that healing is a journey we don't have to take alone. This understanding allows me to support my clients not just in achieving their goals, but in finding the strength and courage to thrive even in adversity.

By finding ways to heal, I not only honored our baby's memory but also became stronger for my family—and for those I coach. This resilience continues to shape how I approach challenges, reminding me that even in the face of loss, there is always a path forward.

The lessons I learned through my journey of loss and healing have deepened my understanding of what resilience truly means. It is not just about surviving hardships but about embracing the growth, strength, and clarity that can come from them. To fully appreciate resilience, it's important to define what it is—and what it is not. By grounding our understanding in expert perspectives, we can better recognize the dynamic and transformative nature of resilience.

Let's explore this concept in more depth.

Defining Resilience: What It Is and What It Is Not

Resilience is often misunderstood as simply the ability to "bounce back" from adversity. While it does involve recovery, true resilience is a dynamic process that incorporates emotional flexibility, mental strength, and purposeful growth. Drawing from the insights of the American Psychological Association (APA), Rick Hanson's *Resilient: How to Grow an Unshakable Core of Calm, Strength, and Happiness,* and George Mason University's model on resilience (the Mason Resilience Model; see also chapters 4, 5, and 8), we can clarify what resilience is—and what it is not.

What Resilience Is

1. The Ability to Adapt

According to the APA, resilience is "the process and outcome of successfully adapting to difficult or challenging life experiences, especially through mental, emotional, and behavioral flexibility and adjustment to external and internal demands." It involves flexibility in how we approach challenges, shifting strategies when necessary, and maintaining a focus on recovery and well-being (APA, 2014).

2. An Inner Resource for Growth

Hanson emphasizes that resilience is not just about surviving hard times but thriving through them. Resilience strengthens our ability to remain calm and steady, even in adversity, helping us to grow stronger and more self-aware over time (Hanson, 2018).

3. A Holistic Model of Strength

The Mason Resilience Model highlights resilience as a blend of emotional, cognitive, physical, and social strengths. Key components include fostering positive emotions, building social support, and finding meaning in life to stay grounded and purposeful. Resilience also relies on effective coping strategies and maintaining physical well-being, which enhances our ability to manage stress and recover from challenges. Together, these elements create a holistic framework, empowering us to not only endure adversity but thrive through it.

4. A Learnable Skill

Resilience is a skill that can be cultivated, not an innate quality. Hanson describes resilience as a collection of inner strengths— compassion, grit, calm, courage, mindfulness, gratitude, motivation, aspiration, learning, confidence, intimacy, and generosity—that we can actively grow through consistent practice and self-awareness (Hanson, 2018).

5. Dynamic and Ongoing

Resilience, not static or one-size-fits-all, evolves with life experiences, learning, and effort (APA, 2014). The APA highlights that resilience develops gradually, shaped by how we navigate and grow from the difficulties we encounter.

What Resilience Is Not

1. The Absence of Stress or Difficulty

Resilience is not about avoiding challenges or pain. According to the Mason Resilience Model, adversity and setbacks are part of life. Moreover, resilience is the process of navigating through, not around, these setbacks.

2. Suppressing or Ignoring Emotions

Resilience does not mean bottling up feelings or pretending everything is okay. It includes acknowledging pain, working through emotions, and finding constructive ways to cope and grow. The APA highlights that resilience depends on how you interact and adapt.

3. A Quick Fix

Resilience is not an immediate return to "normal." It is a gradual process of healing, learning, and rebuilding. Hanson's work emphasizes patience and self-compassion, recognizing that growth takes time (Hanson, 2018).

4. An Individual Effort

The Mason Resilience Model stresses the importance of community, connection, and support systems in building resilience. It is not a solo journey but one enriched by relationships and shared experiences.

Bringing It Together

Resilience is a deeply human quality, one that combines strength, flexibility, and the ability to grow from adversity. It's about facing life's challenges with an open heart, a steady mind, and a willingness to adapt. As Hanson explains, resilience is like building an internal bank of resources, ensuring you have the emotional, mental, and social tools needed to weather life's storms and emerge stronger.

More than just a concept, resilience is a quality that shapes how we endure, recover, and grow through life's challenges. As we bring together the foundational understanding of resilience—what it is and what it is not—we begin to see it as both an art and a practice. But to truly grasp the essence of resilience, it helps to visualize it in action. A powerful metaphor for resilience lies in the image of a spring: adaptable yet unbreakable.

Let's delve into this analogy to deepen our understanding of how resilience operates in our daily lives.

The Spring That Bends but Doesn't Break

Unyielding strength is another way resilience is often misunderstood, but true resilience is more nuanced. It's not about being rigid or unaffected by challenges; rather, it's about adaptability and recovery. Think of a spring. When pressure is applied, the spring compresses, bending and adapting to the force. But when the pressure is released, it returns to its original shape, unbroken and ready for whatever comes next. This is the essence of resilience.

Much like the spring, resilience is the ability to absorb life's pressures, adjust as needed, and then bounce back. Life's challenges may temporarily reshape us, but resilience ensures we don't lose our core strength. It allows us to bend without breaking, to be flexible without compromising our integrity, and to return stronger, more capable, and ready to face future demands.

As we reflect on the metaphor of the spring, it's essential to consider how resilience shows up in our own lives. What pressures have tested our strength, and how have we adapted to them? How can we continue to build the capacity to bend without breaking?

In the next section, you'll find a set of reflection questions designed to help you explore your own resilience. These prompts will guide you to uncover patterns, identify strengths, and consider areas for growth as you continue to develop your inner spring.

Let's take a moment to reflect and discover.

Reflection

Building Your Resilience

Resilience is a skill that grows through reflection, intentionality, and practice. By taking time to explore your personal experiences, beliefs, and habits, you can uncover valuable insights into how resilience shows up in your life. Take some time for yourself in a quiet space, with a journal in hand and an open mind. As you explore the following questions, focus on being truthful and curious about your thoughts and feelings. This activity is designed to guide you through a process of self-discovery, helping you to think deeply about resilience, evaluate your current approach to challenges, and identify actionable steps to strengthen your ability to bounce back.

Let's dive into these reflection questions to build your personalized roadmap for resilience.

Think (Understanding & Awareness)

Consider these questions to explore your current understanding:

1. How do you define resilience in your own words?
2. What challenges in your life have required the most resilience?
3. How does your mindset influence your ability to bounce back from setbacks?
4. What emotions are most common for you during times of adversity?
5. How do you define failure, and what role does it play in your personal growth?

Evaluate (Analyzing & Reflecting)

Take time to analyze and reflect on your emotional habits and patterns:

1. How have past failures shaped your understanding of resilience?
2. Reflect on a time when resilience helped you overcome a major obstacle. What did you learn?
3. What beliefs or habits might be holding you back from developing resilience?
4. How do you currently respond to stress or adversity?
5. In what ways can you shift your perspective to view challenges as opportunities?

Act (Implementation & Practice)

Turn your reflections into action with these practical steps:

1. What practices can you implement to build resilience in your daily life?
2. How can you use physical activity or relaxation techniques to strengthen resilience?
3. What is one strategy you'll use to reframe failures as learning experiences?
4. How can you proactively prepare for challenges in your personal or professional life?
5. What positive habit will you commit to for fostering resilience this week?

As you reflect on your personal experiences and insights from the previous activity, you've begun to uncover the unique ways resilience shapes your life. Now, it's time to take those reflections a step further by creating a personalized "resilience recipe." This next activity will help you translate your thoughts into actionable practices by identifying key ingredients—emotional, social, mental, and physical—that contribute to your resilience.

Let's bring it all together and craft a practical plan to strengthen and sustain your resilience moving forward.

Activity:
Resilience Recipe

If you've completed your reflection, you're ready to turn your insights into action. In this activity, you'll focus on transforming your reflections on resilience into a practical plan. Using the components of the Mason Resilience Model, you'll craft your personalized resilience recipe—a tailored plan to help you navigate and thrive through life's challenges.

Take a look at the sample resilience recipe below for inspiration. Use it as a guide to craft a recipe that aligns with your unique needs and strengths. By the end of this activity, you'll have your own resilience recipe—a practical, personalized tool to support you in building and sustaining resilience in your daily life.

Let's get started!

Title: My Resilience Recipe

Servings: Enough to support resilience through life's challenges

Ingredients:

- 1 cup of *positive emotions*: (e.g., Practicing daily gratitude journaling)
- 2 tablespoons of *social support*: (e.g., Weekly coffee with a friend)
- A generous pinch of *meaning in life*: (e.g., Reflecting on my core values monthly)
- A dash of *coping*: (e.g., Five-minute mindfulness practices during stressful moments)
- A sprinkle of *physical well-being*: (e.g., Evening walks three times a week).

Reflect on Each Category

Below are the five components of the Mason Resilience Model. For each, reflect on the practices, habits, or strategies that currently support you—or that you'd like to incorporate. Use the prompts provided to guide your thoughts.

1. Positive Emotions:

Positive emotions are brief responses that bring joy, hope, or gratitude. These feelings help you see challenges more clearly and foster emotional balance.

- What activities or moments bring you joy, gratitude, or hope?
- How can you incorporate more of these positive emotions into your daily life?

Examples: Practicing gratitude journaling, enjoying a hobby, spending time in nature.

2. Social Support:

Social support is about feeling connected to others and knowing you can rely on them for advice or encouragement.

- Who in your life provides emotional or practical support?
- How do you strengthen and maintain these relationships?

Examples: Scheduling regular time with loved ones, joining a supportive community, or seeking mentorship.

3. Meaning in Life:

Meaning in life is about understanding your purpose and making sense of your place in the world.

What gives your life purpose?

How do you remind yourself of your goals and values?

Examples: Setting meaningful goals, volunteering, or reflecting on your values regularly.

4. Coping:

Coping refers to how you manage stress and regulate your thoughts, emotions, and actions during difficult times.

- What strategies help you manage stress effectively?
- How do you reset after a tough day?

Examples: Practicing mindfulness, reframing negative thoughts, or engaging in calming activities like yoga.

5. Physical Well-Being:

Physical well-being involves maintaining your objective health (e.g., exercise, diet, sleep).

- What habits contribute to your physical health?
- How do you listen to your body and prioritize self-care?

Examples: Walking daily, preparing healthy meals, or sticking to a consistent sleep schedule.

Identify Your Core Ingredients

Review your reflections and select one to two ingredients from each category that feel most relevant and impactful for your life right now.

Write Your Recipe

Use the template below to craft your personalized resilience recipe and describe how you will incorporate these practices into your daily or weekly routine.

Title: My Resilience Recipe

Servings: Enough to support resilience through life's challenges

Ingredients:

- 1 cup of *positive emotions*:

- 2 tablespoons of *social support*:

- A generous pinch of *meaning in life*:

- A dash of *coping*:

- A sprinkle of *physical well-being*:

Reflect on Your Recipe

Answer the following questions:

- How does this recipe help you build resilience?
- What small steps can you take this week to bring your recipe to life?

Revisit and Adjust

Like any recipe, your resilience formula may need tweaks over time. Revisit it every three months to evaluate what's working, what's not, and what new ingredients you might want to add.

Closing Chapter 2: Resilience- The Art of Bouncing Back

Throughout this chapter, we've explored resilience from multiple angles: understanding its true essence, reflecting on personal experiences, and creating practical strategies to strengthen it.

As you move forward, remember that resilience is not about avoiding hardship but embracing the opportunities for growth it presents. Resilience is more than a skill—it's a way of life, a mindset that empowers us to adapt, grow, and thrive in the face of life's challenges. Whether through moments of reflection, building your resilience recipe, or leaning into the metaphor of the spring that bends but doesn't break, the tools you cultivate will serve as anchors in even the toughest storms.

In the next chapter, we'll move our focus to another cornerstone of emotional intelligence: the art of tuning into your inner voice. Just as resilience provides the strength to recover, your inner voice guides the choices and direction of your journey. Together, these elements form a foundation for navigating life's complexities with clarity, purpose, and balance. If another chapter resonates more deeply with where you are right now, feel free to navigate there—this journey is yours to shape.

Let's take the next step on this empowering journey.

Chapter 3

Tuning into Your Inner Voice

- SELF-TALK AND INNER DIALOGUE
- REFLECTION: TUNING INTO YOUR INNER VOICE
- ACTIVITY: RESHAPE THE NARRATIVE

3

Tuning Into Your Inner Voice

"All that we are is the result of what we have thought: It is founded on our thoughts, it is made up of our thoughts."
Buddha

Have you ever caught yourself thinking, *I'm not good enough* or *I'll never figure this out*? Maybe it was during a tough conversation, a moment of failure, or when life felt overwhelmingly uncertain. Those fleeting thoughts, often unnoticed, have the power to shape how we see ourselves and the world.

Our inner voice holds the power to shape how we see ourselves and the world around us. It influences how we interpret challenges, process emotions, and move forward from difficult experiences. Sometimes, however, the narratives we create can leave us feeling stuck or powerless. It's in these moments that the practice of reframing becomes essential.

This chapter embodies a simple truth: Our thoughts shape our reality. Buddha's words remind us that the narrative we create within ourselves has the power to define our actions, our emotions, and ultimately our sense of self. But what happens when those narratives turn negative? How do we tune into a kinder, more constructive inner dialogue?

To illustrate this, let me share a personal story—an experience that tested my resilience and taught me the transformative power of rewriting the narrative I told myself.

Reframing My Inner Narrative: The Day Resilience Took the Wheel

It was a cold, rainy day, and as first-time homebuyers deep in the throes of renovations, my husband and I had made yet another trip to the local home improvement store. He pulled into a parking spot right in front of the store, planning to run in quickly to grab the last few items needed to complete our project. Leaving the engine running to keep the heat on, he stepped out of the car and disappeared into the store.

I sat in the backseat, next to my infant daughter, who was bundled up in her car seat. The sound of the rain hitting the roof was steady, almost comforting, as I watched people come and go. Then, out of the corner of my eye, I noticed a man approaching the car. He was walking directly toward the driver's side door, closer than seemed normal. At first, I thought it was odd but not alarming—until he opened the door, got in, closed it, and started to shift the car into reverse.

My mind struggled to comprehend what was happening. *Is this real? Is someone actually trying to steal the car?* Then, the questions flooded in: *What is he going to do? Will he hurt us? Will my daughter be okay?* The seconds felt like hours as a surge of adrenaline coursed through my body. Before I could even think, I was screaming at the top of my lungs and reaching over the seat to grab him, fighting to get him out of the car.

He froze, startled by my reaction. Later, I learned he thought the car was empty. In the next instant, he flung open the door and bolted. Shaking, I immediately called my husband, frantically explaining what had just happened. He ran out of the store with the sales associate who had been helping him, and together they cornered the man as the police arrived.

In the aftermath, I struggled with an overwhelming sense of fear and vulnerability. I couldn't shake the feeling that I had lost my sense of safety, even in broad daylight. The memory of that day lingered, and for a long time, I found myself replaying the incident, describing it in ways that amplified my feelings of helplessness.

Original Narrative:

"I was a victim of a carjacking. Someone tried to steal my car while my baby and I were inside. I feel like I've lost my sense of safety and control over my life."

This way of thinking left me feeling like a prisoner to the experience, unable to move past it. The more I told the story this way, the more I felt trapped by it. It wasn't until years later that I realized I needed to change the way I spoke about that day—not just to others, but to myself. Reframing my inner narrative became a turning point.

Through intentional work and mindfulness, I began to shift the way I viewed the experience. I started to see it not just as something that had happened to me, but as something I had survived and grown from. This reframing wasn't easy, but it was powerful. I went from a narrative rooted in victimhood to one that celebrated my resilience and strength.

New Narrative:

"I survived a traumatic carjacking. Despite the fear, I found the strength to fight back and protect my daughter. This experience showed me how resilient I am and taught me the importance of vigilance. I've taken proactive measures to enhance our safety and now feel more empowered. Through mindfulness and grounding techniques, I've learned to calm my mind and body and face life with a renewed sense of strength. Breathe."

Reframing my inner narrative didn't erase the fear or the memory of that day, but it allowed me to take control of the story. By changing the way I spoke to myself, I reclaimed my sense of safety and power. I previously viewed the long-term mental and emotional distress caused by the event as a tragedy. However, I no longer see it that way;

I see it as a testament to my resilience, my determination, and my ability to adapt and thrive even in the face of fear.

This experience taught me that our true essence lies not in what happens to us, but in how we choose to respond. It's a lesson that has profoundly shaped my life and my coaching, empowering me to approach challenges with a renewed perspective and a resilient spirit.

This journey of reframing my inner narrative highlights a universal truth: The stories we tell ourselves hold immense power. They shape how we perceive our past, engage with the present, and prepare for the future. At the heart of this transformation lies the inner dialogue we have every day—our self-talk. Understanding and mastering this internal narrative is key to building resilience, fostering growth, and unlocking our full potential. Let's delve deeper into the nature of self-talk and explore how it influences every aspect of our lives.

Self-Talk and Inner Dialogue: The Stories We Tell Ourselves

Self-talk—the internal narrative that plays in our minds—is a powerful force shaping how we view ourselves, others, and the world. It has the capacity to either propel us forward or hold us back, influencing our confidence, actions, and resilience. The key lies in understanding its nature, recognizing its patterns, and transforming it into a tool for growth (Hanson, 2018).

The Power and Pitfalls of Self-Talk

At its core, self-talk reflects our beliefs, values, and perceptions. Positive self-talk builds resilience and fosters a growth mindset—the belief that abilities and intelligence can develop through effort and learning (Dweck, 2006). For instance, when faced with a challenge, self-talk like "I can learn from this" strengthens our ability to persevere. On the other hand, negative self-talk, often rooted in the brain's natural negativity bias, reinforces limiting beliefs: "I always fail; why even try?"

The negativity bias, an evolutionary trait designed to help us avoid danger, tends to make negative thoughts and experiences stick more readily than positive ones (Hanson, 2018). While this bias once served to protect us, it can now amplify self-criticism and doubt. For example, we may replay a single mistake repeatedly, overshadowing countless successes. This pattern can erode confidence and hinder our ability to embrace challenges with curiosity and optimism.

Reframing Inner Dialogue with a Growth Mindset

A growth mindset, a concept popularized by psychologist Carol Dweck, offers a transformative way to approach self-talk. It encourages us to see challenges not as insurmountable barriers but as opportunities for learning and development (Dweck, 2006). When self-talk aligns with a growth mindset, it becomes a source of motivation: "I'm struggling now, but I can improve with practice and persistence."

Cultivating this mindset requires intentionality and practice. I find the Notice-Shift-Rewire method, introduced by Nate Klemp, PhD, and Eric Langshur in their book *Start Here: Master the Lifelong Habit of Wellbeing* to be a valuable tool. This three-step method helps break the cycle of negative self-talk and establish a healthier inner dialogue (Klemp & Langshur, 2017).

1. **Notice:** Pay attention to the negative or self-limiting thought patterns as they arise.

   Example: "I'm not good enough for this task."

2. **Shift:** Consciously redirect your focus to a more empowering perspective.
3. **Reframe:** "This is difficult, but I have the skills to figure it out."
4. **Rewire:** Solidify this new thought by reflecting on it, repeating it, and allowing it to shape your response.
5. **Reinforce:** "I've overcome similar challenges before, and I can do it again."

By practicing this or similar methods, you create new mental pathways that prioritize positivity and growth over doubt and fear.

Inner Dialogue and Emotional Well-Being

Inner dialogue extends beyond self-talk to encompass the ongoing conversation we have about our identity, worth, and abilities. Negative inner dialogue often stems from past experiences or internalized messages, leading to rigid narratives that limit growth. For instance, "I've always been bad at math" might prevent someone from even trying to improve (Dweck, 2006).

A growth-oriented dialogue might look like this:

- **Original Thought:** *"I've always failed at this; why bother?"*
- **Reframed Thought:** *"This is a chance to learn and grow. I can take small steps to improve."*

Over time, this process builds resilience, confidence, and emotional balance (Hanson, 2018).

The Ripple Effect of Self-Talk

The impact of self-talk and inner dialogue goes far beyond our minds. Negative self-talk can lead to self-doubt, procrastination, and fear of failure, creating a cycle of avoidance (Hanson, 2018). Conversely, positive self-talk promotes persistence, optimism, and a willingness to take risks. It ripples into our relationships, professional endeavors, and ability to handle adversity.

For example, someone who replaces "I'm terrible at public speaking" with "I can practice and improve my presentation skills" is more likely to embrace opportunities for growth. This shift empowers them to take action rather than retreat, leading to meaningful progress (Dweck, 2006).

Practicing Mindful Self-Talk

The journey toward healthier self-talk begins with mindfulness. Observing thoughts without judgment creates space to choose responses that align with a growth mindset (Klemp & Langshur, 2017). Incorporating mindfulness and self-compassion into daily routines reinforces these changes. Techniques like journaling, gratitude exercises, or taking moments to pause and breathe strengthen positive self-talk and counteract negativity bias (Hanson, 2018). Over time, these practices help reframe not only individual thoughts but also the broader narrative we carry about ourselves.

Why This Matters

Our inner dialogue shapes our emotional well-being, decisions, and resilience. It's the foundation for navigating challenges and achieving personal growth. By understanding and transforming self-talk, we can cultivate a mindset that empowers rather than limits us.

As we move forward, reflect on your own self-talk. What patterns do you notice? How does your inner dialogue align with a growth mindset? Let's continue this journey toward tuning into your inner voice and unlocking your full potential.

As we delve deeper into the art of transforming self-talk, it's essential to recognize the profound impact of our inner narratives. They are not just background noise; they are the soundtrack of our lives, influencing every step we take. What if we could take control of this internal music, curating a playlist that energizes and uplifts us rather than one that drags us down?

To explore this idea further, let's consider an analogy that perfectly captures the power and potential of our inner dialogue: the DJ of your mind. Just as a DJ can change the mood of a room with a single track, you can shift your mindset and transform your outlook by reframing the stories you tell yourself.

The DJ of Your Mind: Reframing the Soundtrack of Your Thoughts

Imagine your inner voice as the DJ of your mind, spinning the soundtrack that sets the mood for your life. This DJ curates the songs—your thoughts—that play on repeat throughout your day. Some tracks inspire confidence, joy, and determination, while others replay the heavy beats of self-doubt, fear, and negativity. Just as a DJ shapes the vibe of a party, your inner voice influences the energy of your mindset, actions, and emotional well-being.

The beauty of this analogy is that it highlights your authority. If you don't like the tune your inner DJ is playing, you have the power to change it. Reframing your narrative isn't about ignoring difficult realities or pretending everything is perfect—it's about consciously choosing to replace harmful patterns with constructive, empowering ones.

Recognizing the Tracks: Awareness of Self-Talk

The first step to changing the tune is recognizing what's currently playing. What does your mental playlist sound like? Does it uplift you or weigh you down? Often, our inner DJ has a negativity bias, favoring tracks that amplify fear, self-criticism, and doubt. This negativity bias, as psychologists explain, is an evolutionary mechanism designed to help us focus on potential threats but can lead to an unbalanced view of ourselves and the world (Hanson, 2018).

These negative tracks often stem from past experiences, societal pressures, or deeply ingrained beliefs. Like a DJ stuck in a loop, the same harmful narratives can play over and over, shaping how we see ourselves and approach challenges.

Changing the Tune: Reframing the Narrative

The power to reframe lies in your ability to interrupt this mental playlist and introduce new tracks. Much like a DJ can shift from a slow, somber ballad to an upbeat anthem, you can choose thoughts that promote a growth mindset and emotional resilience.

For example:

- **Instead of:** "I failed at this before, so I'll fail again," reframe with: "I've learned from my past attempts, and I'm better equipped to try again."
- **Instead of:** "I'm not good at this," reframe with: "I'm still learning, and progress takes time."

Reframing doesn't erase challenges or emotions—it gives you the ability to process them in a way that fosters growth and forward momentum.

Curating a Positive Playlist

Building a better mental playlist takes intentional effort. Here are some practical strategies to help your inner DJ curate empowering tracks:

1. Identify the *negative tracks*: Pay attention to repetitive negative thoughts or phrases that undermine your confidence or joy.

2. Interrupt the *loop*: When you notice a harmful narrative, pause and challenge its validity. Ask yourself, "Is this thought helpful? Is it true? (Klemp & Langshur, 2017)."

3. Replace the *track*: Introduce a more constructive thought that aligns with a growth mindset. If self-doubt creeps in, remind yourself of past successes or strengths.

4. Celebrate *progress*: Recognize and affirm when you successfully shift your narrative. Positive reinforcement strengthens the habit of choosing empowering thoughts.

Tune In and Take Control

The music in your mind plays constantly, shaping your perception and actions. The question is: Are you letting your inner DJ play the same tired, negative tracks, or are you taking control of the playlist? As we move forward in this chapter, we'll explore practical ways to fine-tune your self-talk and cultivate an inner dialogue that supports your growth, resilience, and well-being.

Now that you understand the power of your inner DJ, it's time to take a closer look at the tracks playing on repeat in your mind. What messages dominate your self-talk? Are they empowering or limiting? Reflection is the first step in reshaping your internal soundtrack. In the next activity, you'll have the opportunity to tune in to your inner dialogue, identify patterns, and begin curating a playlist of thoughts that uplift and strengthen you.

Let's dive in and start creating the mindset that will help you thrive.

Reflection

Tuning into Your Inner Voice

Your inner voice is a constant companion, shaping how you see yourself, navigate challenges, and how you connect with the world. By tuning into this dialogue, you can uncover the beliefs and patterns influencing your emotions, decisions, and overall well-being. Grab a notebook, settle into a calm place, and open your mind to self-reflection. This activity is designed to help you pause and reflect on your self-talk, assess its impact, and take actionable steps to align your inner dialogue with a more compassionate, empowering narrative. Through thoughtful questions, you'll gain awareness of your current mindset, identify areas for growth, and create habits to foster a supportive and resilient inner voice.

Let's take this opportunity to listen deeply, reflect intentionally, and make meaningful changes to the soundtrack of your thoughts.

Think (Understanding & Awareness)

Consider these questions to explore your current understanding:

1. What does mindfulness mean to you, and how does it shape your thoughts?
2. How would you describe your current inner dialogue?
3. What triggers negative self-talk in your daily life?
4. What role do mindfulness and self-talk play in your emotional well-being?
5. How do you think your inner voice influences your actions and decisions?

Evaluate (Analyzing & Reflecting)

Take time to analyze and reflect on your emotional habits and patterns:

1. Reflect on a moment when your inner voice positively influenced your decision-making.
2. What patterns do you notice in your self-talk during stressful situations?
3. How do your thoughts impact the way you react to challenges?
4. In what ways has your inner dialogue shaped your self-confidence?
5. How often do you pause to assess the narrative you tell yourself?

Act (Implementation & Practice)

Turn your reflections into action with these practical steps:

1. What mindful practices (meditation, journaling) can you incorporate to shape your inner voice?
2. How can you reframe a recurring negative thought into a positive one?
3. What daily habit can help you monitor and manage self-talk?
4. How will you practice self-compassion when you notice negative self-talk?
5. What action will you take this week to make your inner voice more supportive?

As you complete the reflection questions, you may notice patterns in your self-talk and how they influence your emotions and decisions. Understanding these patterns is the first step toward growth, but the real transformation comes when you take what you've learned and actively reshape the narrative you tell yourself.

In the next activity, we'll take this deeper. By reflecting on a specific challenge, you'll explore your feelings, uncover hidden lessons, and reframe the story in a way that highlights your resilience and strength.

Let's move forward and begin crafting a narrative that empowers you to thrive.

Activity

Reshape the Narrative

The stories we tell ourselves about challenging experiences shape how we view ourselves and our potential. This activity will guide you to reflect on a difficult event, acknowledge your feelings, uncover hidden lessons, and rewrite your narrative with a focus on growth and resilience. This is not about ignoring hardships but reframing them to highlight your strength and adaptability. By the end, you'll have a renewed story that empowers you to move forward with confidence. Feel free to write your responses in the space provided or use a journal for deeper reflection.

Let's begin.

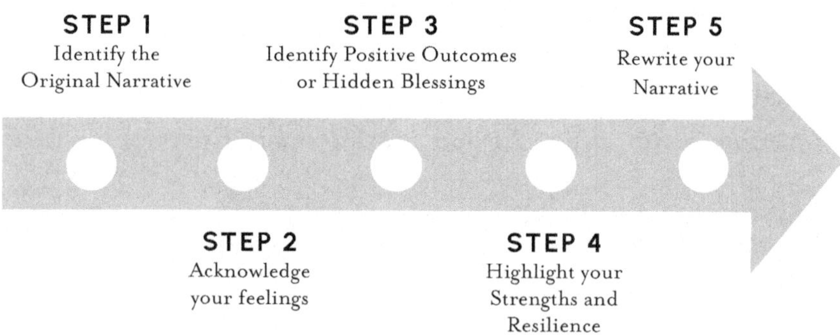

Step 1: Identify the Original Narrative

Write down a brief description of a challenging experience you have faced.

Example: "I had been working hard to secure a leadership position at my company and was a top candidate for a promotion. However, after a final round of interviews, I learned that the position was offered to someone else. I felt overlooked and doubted my abilities as a leader."

Your Narrative:

____

____

____

____

____

____

Step 2: Acknowledge Your Feelings

Write down how the experience made you feel.

Example: "I felt frustrated, undervalued, and disheartened."

Your Feelings:

____

____

____

____

____

Step 3: Identify Positive Outcomes or Hidden Gems

Think about any positive outcomes, lessons learned, or hidden gems that resulted from this experience.

Example: "I didn't get the promotion, but this allowed me to take on a special project that expanded my skills. A year later, this experience helped me secure an even better leadership position in a new company, where I felt more aligned with the culture and vision."

Your Positive Outcomes/Hidden Gems:

____

____

____

____

____

Step 4: Highlight Your Strengths and Resilience

Reflect on how you showed strength and resilience during or after the experience.

Example: "Instead of giving up, I chose to use the experience as a learning opportunity. I worked on my leadership skills, sought feedback, and stayed committed to growth. This helped me realize my value and find success on a different path."

Your Strengths and Resilience:

Step 5: Rewrite Your Narrative

Using the insights from Steps 1 - 4, rewrite your original narrative to focus on your journey of growth and resilience.

Example: "I worked hard for a promotion that I believed I deserved, but the position was given to another candidate. At first, I felt frustrated and disheartened. However, this experience became a turning point. It pushed me to reflect on my goals, enhance my skills, and pursue opportunities that aligned with my long-term aspirations. Ultimately, this setback led me to a leadership role in a company where I thrive and feel valued. Not getting the original position turned out to be a stepping stone toward an even better opportunity."

Your Rewritten Narrative:

Reflect on the process of reshaping your narrative.

How do you feel now about the experience? How has your perspective changed?

Your Reflection:

____

____

____

____

____

Closing Chapter 3: Tuning into Your Inner Voice

Your inner voice is the compass guiding how you navigate the world. It influences your choices, your resilience, and your ability to grow from life's challenges. By tuning into this dialogue and actively reshaping it, you unlock the power to transform self-doubt into confidence, setbacks into opportunities, and everyday moments into stepping stones toward personal growth.

However, it's important to recognize that these strategies are not a panacea. This is not about ignoring pain or pretending everything is fine when it's not. You must engage with each step at a pace that feels mentally and emotionally manageable for you. For example, when grieving the loss of a loved one, you may not be ready for months—or even longer—to lean into positive thoughts or reframe your inner dialogue. And that's okay. Resilience is not about rushing through healing but about allowing yourself the time and space to process and adapt when you're truly ready.

In this chapter, we explored the profound impact of self-talk and inner dialogue. Through reflection and reframing, we discovered how to shift negative narratives into empowering ones that fuel resilience and positivity. These practices are not just tools for personal well-being but also catalysts for how you show up in relationships, work, and every corner of your life. Remember, reshaping your inner voice is a journey, not a race, and honoring where you are in the process is a vital part of the path forward.

Next up is Chapter 4, we'll take this internal work and examine how it influences the way we connect with others. Just as your inner voice shapes your self-perception, your interactions and relationships are built on the foundation of that inner dialogue. Alternatively, think of this book like a Choose Your Own Adventure—feel free to jump to the chapter that resonates with you.

Let's explore how to cultivate empathy, trust, and meaningful connections by aligning your inner and outer worlds.

Chapter 4

The Harmony of Relationships

- SOCIAL SUPPORT AND SOCIAL SKILLS
- REFLECTION: BUILDING HARMONIOUS RELATIONSHIPS
- ACTIVITY: CONNECTION TREE

4

The Harmony of Relationships

"Connection is why we're here; it is what gives purpose and meaning to our lives."
—Brené Brown

What's the most meaningful connection you've ever experienced? Was it a friendship, a partnership, or perhaps a fleeting moment with someone who left a lasting impact? Relationships are more than just interactions—they challenge us to grow, inspire us to be better, and provide the support we need to navigate life's trials.

Brené Brown's insight beautifully underscores the central role that relationships play in enriching our lives. Whether personal or professional, meaningful connections are built on the pillars of emotional intelligence—empathy, communication, and trust. More than just a part of life, they are the bedrock that supports our growth, helps us flourish, and gives our lives meaning.

To truly understand the harmony and strength that relationships can provide, I want to share a deeply personal story about how I found my home within a prestigious federal agency. It's a story of how a single, impactful connection changed the trajectory of my journey, my career, reminding me of the transformative power of building relationships rooted in trust and authenticity.

The Harmony of Relationships: A Personal Journey

Relationships shape not only who we are but also who we aspire to become. One relationship in particular stands out in my journey—a mentorship that not only transformed my professional path but also reaffirmed the power of connection, insight, and encouragement.

While working in the private sector, I was fortunate to be part of a high-potential program which paired me with a senior vice president in my organization. She was a powerhouse of wisdom and experience, and I always looked forward to our mentoring conversations. They weren't just about tasks or projects; they were about vision and purpose. Every conversation left me feeling empowered, as if a part of me that I didn't fully understand was being awakened.

During one of our sessions, she said something that stopped me in my tracks: "You have a project management certification, a PHR, SHRM, and Six Sigma certification. Have you ever thought about doing Organizational Development and coaching full-time?" Her words struck a chord deep within me. I had always loved Organizational Development; it had been a natural and fulfilling part of my roles over the years. But I had never considered transitioning into that world fully. It was like she had seen something in me that I hadn't yet allowed myself to see.

The timing was uncanny. That same week, as if the universe itself had conspired, a job alert landed in my inbox. It was an Organizational Development and coaching position at a prestigious federal agency. My first thought was, *Is this really happening? Could this be fate?* With her encouragement echoing in my mind, I decided to take a leap of faith. I applied for the job, poured my heart into the process, and landed the role.

Since then, my journey with the agency has been nothing short of extraordinary. The role stretched me, challenged me, and allowed me to contribute to a mission that impacts the world. It also inspired me to start my own coaching and consulting business, Acnestis Coaching & Consulting, LLC. Helping others and teams become the best versions of themselves has been one of the most rewarding chapters of my life. Through these experiences, I've come to appreciate how essential relationships are in shaping our potential and guiding us toward paths we may not have seen for ourselves.

Looking back, I feel deeply grateful for my mentor. She saw something greater in me and helped me navigate the complexities of my professional life. But more than that, she helped me see the bigger picture—not just of my career, but of my capacity to contribute, grow, and inspire others. Her belief in me was a catalyst, but it was my ability to foster social support and my social skills that enabled me to fully embrace the opportunity.

This experience has taught me that relationships are not just about guidance or advice. They're about harmony—a dynamic interplay where insights are shared, potential is recognized, and dreams are encouraged. Mentorship, in particular, is a symphony of empowerment, where one person's faith in another can transform lives.

As I reflect on this chapter of my life, I am reminded of the incredible power we hold in each other's lives. Whether as coach, mentors, friends, family, or colleagues, our relationships are opportunities to build, uplift, and inspire. They are the harmony that helps us compose the music of our lives.

In the chapters to come, I hope you'll reflect on the relationships in your life—the ones that inspire, challenge, and propel you forward. Just as my mentor did for me, consider how you can be that source of encouragement and clarity for someone else. After all, in the symphony of life, the harmony of relationships is what makes the journey truly beautiful.

As we transition from exploring the transformative power of mentorship to understanding the broader framework of emotional intelligence in relationships, it's clear that meaningful connections are built on both support and skill. Mentorship illustrates the profound impact of social support, while fostering harmony in relationships requires a blend of empathy, communication, and adaptability.

In the next section, we'll delve into the essential components of building emotionally intelligent relationships, focusing on the roles of social support and social skills as the cornerstones for personal and professional growth.

Building Emotional Intelligence in Personal and Professional Relationships: Social Support and Social Skills

Relationships are an essential foundation of emotional intelligence, influencing how we navigate both personal and professional landscapes. Two key components in building emotionally intelligent relationships are social support and social skills. Together, these create a framework for nurturing trust, collaboration, and mutual growth.

The Role of Social Support

Social support, as defined by the Mason Resilience Model (see also chapters 2, 5, and 8), is "the degree to which a person feels they can rely on or turn to other people for support, advice, or encouragement." It underscores the importance of having a network of individuals (e.g., spouse, friends, family, neighbors, religious institutions) who provide emotional, informational, and practical resources during times of need. This support system not only helps us cope with challenges but also enhances our emotional resilience, creating a safety net that fosters well-being.

For example, in professional settings, a strong network of colleagues can offer advice, share knowledge, or lend a listening ear during stressful projects. Similarly, in personal relationships, loved ones can provide encouragement during difficult life transitions, reminding us that we are not alone.

Social Skills: The Bridge to Connection

Daniel Goleman's model of emotional intelligence highlights social skills as a crucial element of managing relationships effectively. Social skills are about guiding interactions in positive directions, whether through leadership, teamwork, or building personal connections. The American Psychological Association elaborates further, describing social skills as including "assertiveness, coping, communication, friendship-making abilities, interpersonal problem-solving, and the capacity to regulate one's thoughts, emotions, and behaviors.

Integrating Social Support and Social Skills

The intersection of social support and social skills creates the foundation for emotionally intelligent relationships. For instance:

- A team leader who recognizes a colleague's stress (social support) and adapts their communication style to offer encouragement (social skills) demonstrates a balanced approach to emotional intelligence.

- In personal relationships, being emotionally available to listen (social support) while resolving conflicts respectfully (social skills) builds lasting bonds.
- In friendships, offering a comforting presence during a difficult time (social support) while using active listening to validate emotions and find common ground (social skills) deepens trust.
- A parent who comforts their child after a failure (social support) while teaching problem-solving strategies in a kind and patient manner (social skills) encourages resilience and self-confidence.

This blend of support and skills is what makes me an effective coach. By leveraging social support, I create a space where individuals feel seen, heard, and empowered to tackle their challenges. Through refined social skills, I guide conversations and actions that inspire growth, improve dynamics, and help others achieve their goals. Coaching, to me, is about harmonizing both elements to help individuals and teams unlock their potential.

Building emotional intelligence in relationships is a dynamic process that requires intentional effort, reflection, and practice. As we cultivate social support and refine our social skills, we create the conditions for greater harmony in both our personal and professional lives. By doing so, we not only improve our own well-being but also contribute to the growth and resilience of those around us.

Our relationships are more than just connections; they are mirrors reflecting who we are and the potential we have yet to discover. My journey with mentorship taught me how powerful it is to have someone who believes in you and helps you see the bigger picture. But these relationships also serve another vital purpose—they help us understand ourselves in ways we couldn't on our own. Just as a label on the outside of a jar holds important information that can't be seen from within, our support system offers insights into our blind spots, strengths, and opportunities. Let's explore how harmonious relationships allow us to gain this outside perspective and foster deeper growth.

Harmonious Relationships: Seeing What's Written on the Jar

Imagine for a moment that you are inside a glass jar with a lid securely fastened. The world is visible around you, but you can't see what's written on the outside of the jar—the label. That label contains crucial information: the ingredients that make you who you are, the values and strengths that fuel you, and the warnings that might signify your vulnerabilities or blind spots. While you may know the contents of the jar to some extent, your perspective is limited by being inside.

This is where harmonious relationships come into play. Your support system—the people who stand outside the jar—can read what you cannot. They see the full label, complete with your strengths, weaknesses, and potential hazards. They can identify the ingredients that energize you, the elements that challenge you, and the areas where you might be blind to your own patterns. This outside perspective is invaluable, especially when navigating life's complexities.

The Power of an Outside Perspective

We all have blind spots. These are the aspects of ourselves that we may not notice or fully understand—our biases, habits, or even unrecognized talents. Being inside the jar, it's nearly impossible to identify these without help. Harmonious relationships, built on trust and emotional intelligence, provide us with people who can hold up a mirror and gently guide us toward greater self-awareness.

For instance:

- A friend may recognize your tendency to overcommit before you do, reminding you to set boundaries and prioritize self-care.
- A mentor might point out untapped skills, urging you to pursue opportunities you hadn't considered.
- A partner or close colleague can offer constructive feedback, helping you refine your approach to a challenge.

Their vantage point allows them to see what you cannot—and their input helps you grow in ways you may not achieve on your own.

Building Trust to Open the Lid

For this system to work, trust is paramount. You have to allow others to lift the lid of the jar and share what they see without defensiveness or fear. Trust is built through consistent communication, mutual respect, and a willingness to be vulnerable. This vulnerability is not a sign of weakness but of strength—acknowledging that we don't have all the answers and that others can offer insights we need.

Think of a time when someone gave you advice that shifted your perspective or helped you overcome a challenge. Their ability to "read the label" for you likely saved you from potential pitfalls or empowered you to seize an opportunity. This dynamic is the essence of harmonious relationships: a balance of giving and receiving insights with the goal of mutual growth.

Reading the Labels for Others

Just as others read the label on your jar, you're able to do the same for them. By developing emotional intelligence, particularly social awareness and empathy, you can support others in uncovering their blind spots and realizing their potential.

This reciprocal dynamic strengthens relationships:

- Empathy allows you to understand the challenges others face and offer insights without judgment.
- Active listening ensures that your feedback is grounded in their needs and context, not your assumptions.
- Encouragement builds their confidence, enabling them to take action based on your perspective.

When both parties commit to this level of connection, relationships transform into partnerships built on trust, understanding, and a shared commitment to growth.

Why Harmonious Relationships Matter

Harmonious relationships extend beyond individual growth; they foster collaboration, innovation, and resilience. In personal life, these connections provide emotional stability and a sense of belonging. In professional settings, they create environments where people thrive, feel valued, and contribute their best work.

Much like the label on the jar provides essential information to the consumer, harmonious relationships provide essential insights for navigating life's complexities. By inviting others to read our labels—and by offering the same in return—we create a network of support that enhances every facet of our lives.

We are all jars, filled with unique ingredients that shape who we are. But no jar is fully self-aware without the help of those standing outside. Harmonious relationships allow us to see beyond our own limitations, empowering us to grow, adapt, and thrive. So, the next time someone offers feedback or encouragement, remember: They're reading your label with care. And in turn, offer to read theirs, because together, we uncover the full picture of what's possible.

Building harmonious relationships requires more than just intention—it demands reflection and action. As we recognize the importance of the people who read our labels and offer perspective, it's essential to turn that insight inward and consider how we show up in our connections. By exploring our patterns, values, and communication styles, we can cultivate deeper, more fulfilling relationships. Let's take the next step in this journey with a reflection activity designed to strengthen our bonds and foster meaningful harmony.

Reflection

Building Harmonious Relationships

Strong and meaningful relationships are at the heart of our personal and professional lives. Yet achieving harmony in these connections requires self-awareness, intentional effort, and a commitment to fostering trust, empathy, and effective communication.

Pick up a notebook, sit in a peaceful setting, and prepare to explore your thoughts with an open heart. This activity is designed to guide you through a process of reflection and action, helping you to better understand the dynamics of your relationships and the role emotional intelligence plays in strengthening them. Through thoughtful questions, you'll explore how your emotions, habits, and interactions shape your connections. You'll also uncover opportunities to build trust, resolve conflicts, and deepen the bonds that matter most. By identifying specific actions you can take, this activity empowers you to actively cultivate harmonious relationships that support your growth and well-being.

Let's dive in and take a step toward creating stronger, more fulfilling connections in your life.

Think (Understanding & Awareness)

Consider these questions to explore your current understanding:

1. How do you define harmony in relationships?
2. What qualities do you value most in meaningful connections?
3. How do your emotions influence the way you communicate with others?
4. What does trust mean to you in both personal and professional relationships?
5. How would you describe your approach to resolving conflicts?

Evaluate (Analyzing & Reflecting)

Take time to analyze and reflect on your emotional habits and patterns:

1. How has emotional intelligence positively impacted a relationship in your life?
2. What role does empathy play in strengthening your connections?

3. How do you handle misunderstandings in your relationships?

4. What patterns or habits might be holding you back from deeper connections?

5. How have past experiences shaped your ability to build trust?

Act (Implementation & Practice)

Turn your reflections into action with these practical steps:

1. What steps can you take to strengthen a key relationship in your life?

2. How will you actively practice empathy in a challenging relationship this week?

3. What communication strategy can you use to resolve a current conflict?

4. How can you show appreciation to someone who supports you?

5. What action will you take to maintain harmony in your closest relationships?

As we reflect on the dynamics of harmonious relationships and the role emotional intelligence plays in strengthening them, it's clear that building meaningful connections requires both intention and action. Understanding the qualities we value, the habits that shape our interactions, and the opportunities that lead to growth will lay the groundwork for deeper bonds. To bring these insights to life, the Connection Tree Activity offers a creative and actionable way to visualize and nurture the relationships that matter most. Let's take what we've learned and begin cultivating a tree of connection, fostering stronger, more fulfilling relationships.

Activity

Connection Tree, Cultivating Meaningful Relationships

Connection is the lifeblood of all meaningful relationships. Whether personal or professional, genuine connection fosters a sense of belonging, understanding, and collaboration. Strong connections don't just happen—they are built through intentional actions, meaningful communication, and consistent care.

The Connection Tree Activity is designed to help you visualize and strengthen the bonds that shape your life. By identifying key relationships and actionable steps to nurture them, this activity empowers you to deepen your connections and foster harmony in your interactions. Grab a journal to record your thoughts as you work through this activity. Let's plant the seeds of connection and watch them flourish!

Steps to Build Your Connection Tree:

1. Add Relationship Branches:

On the tree figure, put your name on the trunk and label each branch with the name of a significant person in your life. These could be family members, friends, colleagues, mentors, or others who play an important role.

2. Reflect on Connection:

For each person, consider the current state of your connection. Use these guiding questions:

- How do I currently show care or attention in this relationship?
- How does this person show their connection to me?
- Are there any opportunities or barriers to deepening this relationship?

3. Identify Actionable Steps:

For each branch, list one specific action you can take to strengthen your connection with that person.

Examples:

- A friend: Schedule a monthly coffee chat to maintain closeness.
- A colleague: Acknowledge their contributions in a team meeting to show appreciation.
- A family member: Set aside time for a heartfelt conversation to catch up and share support.

4. Reflect and Commit:

Look at your completed Connection Tree. Do you notice any recurring themes or patterns in your actions?

Choose 1–2 branches to focus on this week. Commit to taking the identified steps and observe how these actions impact your relationships. Continue with the remaining branches over the course of the next 30 days.

CONNECTION TREE

Closing the Chapter: Harmony of Relationships

As we conclude this chapter on the harmony of relationships, it's clear that meaningful connections are the cornerstone of both our personal and professional growth. Through intentional social support and the development of social skills, we build bonds that not only uplift and inspire but also help us navigate challenges with resilience and strength. Relationships are not just about others—they also reflect our capacity for empathy, trust, and collaboration, reminding us that we are never truly alone in our journeys.

Yet, as we nurture these connections, we must also turn inward. Maintaining harmony in relationships begins with a strong foundation of self-awareness and care. To show up fully for others, we need to prioritize our own well-being. This is where the rhythm of self-care becomes essential—a practice that sustains us, fuels our growth, and allows us to bring our best selves to every interaction.

In the next chapter, we'll explore self-care, which is more than just an act; it's a rhythm we create to balance the demands of life while nurturing our mind, body, and soul. Together, let's discover how cultivating this rhythm can amplify not only our well-being but also the depth and authenticity of our relationships.

If another chapter feels more relevant to you, don't hesitate to skip there.

Chapter 5

Self-Care & Staying Grounded in Chaos

- RESILIENCE ACROSS NEEDS
- REFLECTION: PRIORITIZING PHYSICAL, EMOTIONAL, AND MENTAL HEALTH
- ACTIVITY: 5-4-3-2-1 GROUNDING EXERCISE

5

Self Care & Staying Grounded In Chaos

"Almost everything will work again if you unplug it for a few minutes, including you."
— Anne Lamott

When was the last time you truly paused and gave yourself permission to rest? Have you ever felt like you were running on empty, pushing through each day with nothing left to give? Life can sometimes feel like a relentless whirlwind of responsibilities, deadlines, and expectations, leaving you teetering on the edge of burnout no matter how hard you try to keep up.

Anne Lamott's metaphor reminds us of the necessity of rest and self-care in maintaining our overall well-being. It is like hitting a "Rest" button—not only for our bodies but also for our minds. In this chapter, we will explore the rhythm of self-care and how prioritizing physical, emotional, and mental health is essential for thriving, not just surviving. Self-care is the foundation of resilience and effectiveness. Without it, even the most capable among us can falter under the weight of life's demands. This lesson became all too real for me during a particularly challenging chapter of my life—a time when overcommitment and relentless responsibilities led me to the brink of burnout. Let me share my story, a journey that taught me the true power of staying grounded in chaos.

Personal Story: Self-Care is Not Selfish

Being a military spouse often means constant transitions, from packing up and moving to starting over in a new place, all while creating a sense of stability amidst chaos. When my family relocated from Alabama to Washington, DC, it was one of the most challenging moves yet. The demands of finding employment, childcare, and housing that could support our growing family felt like an uphill battle. To make things even more difficult, my husband was Temporary Duty (TDY) for a couple of months at the beginning of our move, leaving me to handle everything on my own. As if the challenges weren't enough, shortly after being stationed there, we found out we were expecting another child.

With one small child, no family or friends nearby to lean on, and another baby on the way, we had to make tough decisions. I had been offered an incredible opportunity—a strategic HR role—but it came with a catch: The office was 50 miles outside of DC. Meanwhile, my husband had secured a position in the city. After much deliberation, we chose to live outside the city to have more space for our growing family. Once my husband's TDY ended, he began enduring a grueling 90-minute commute each way to and from DC, while I tried to keep everything else afloat. On top of that, he also started a demanding full-time graduate program.

My schedule was packed to the brim. Alongside my HR job, I was adjuncting college courses at two different institutions and managing all the household responsibilities. From grocery shopping and meal prep to full-care hygiene and the physiological needs of my toddler, I took it all on while balancing demanding work schedules. My husband was giving his all with his long commute and job responsibilities, but the weight of it all seemed to fall squarely on my shoulders.

Military spouses often serve too—not in uniform, but in the daily sacrifices, adaptability, and resilience it takes to keep everything running smoothly during times of transition. I felt the weight of that service acutely during this period. My days blurred together—wake up, work, care for the kids, manage the household, and repeat. The physical exhaustion was relentless, but the emotional toll of trying to be everything for everyone was what finally broke me.

One morning, I woke up and couldn't even remember what day it was. My mind was foggy, my energy drained, and I felt like I was running on autopilot. It hit me: *This isn't sustainable*. I was burning out, and if I didn't make changes, I wouldn't be able to show up for myself or my family. That day, I had an honest conversation with my husband. I shared how overwhelmed I felt, and together, we decided it was time to reassess our priorities.

The changes weren't easy, but they were necessary. I started creating boundaries, learning to say "no," and carving out intentional time for myself. I set aside weekly "me time" for walks about a department store alone, listening to music, dancing, reading, or just quiet moments to recharge. We also delegated responsibilities more equitably, and I adjusted my work commitments to focus on what truly mattered.

This experience became a lesson in staying grounded amidst chaos. It reminded me that the demands of life will never stop coming, but how I respond to them makes all the difference. Grounding myself through intentional self-care helped me reclaim a sense of balance and clarity, even in the midst of uncertainty.

That wake-up call transformed how I approached self-care. It taught me that I can't pour from an empty cup and that prioritizing my well-being isn't selfish—it's essential. Staying grounded became my anchor, a way to find calm and stability despite the swirling demands around me. This experience not only helped me find balance but also strengthened my relationship with my husband as we learned to navigate challenges as a team. Most importantly, it reminded me that self-care is the foundation for showing up as the best version of myself for my family, my career, and my life.

This wake-up call reshaped my understanding of self-care and its role in navigating life's inevitable demands. It taught me that prioritizing my physical, emotional, and mental health isn't just an act of self-preservation—it's the cornerstone of resilience. By making intentional changes, I found clarity amidst chaos and reaffirmed my capacity to face challenges with balance and purpose.

With this lesson in mind, it's essential to explore how our foundational needs support well-being and emotional regulation, especially during high-stress situations. It is also useful to understand practical resilience strategies to navigate challenges, maintain balance, and recover from setbacks.

Prioritizing Physical, Emotional, and Mental Health: Resilience Across Maslow's Hierarchy of Needs

Life's challenges often test our limits, requiring us to juggle responsibilities while protecting our well-being. Abraham Maslow's Hierarchy of Needs, introduced in his 1943 paper "A Theory of Human Motivation," provides a framework for understanding how interconnected physical, emotional, and mental health are essential for personal growth. Each level of Maslow's hierarchy depends on resilience—the ability to adapt, recover, and thrive despite setbacks—to meet foundational needs and progress toward self-actualization.

Resilience is the stabilizing force that empowers individuals to overcome disruptions in these needs. Without it, stress and adversity can derail personal growth, leaving individuals unable to advance. By applying strategies that align with both Maslow's framework and the Mason Resilience Model, we can cultivate the strength necessary to sustain well-being, regulate emotions, and achieve fulfillment. Remember, when it comes to resilience strategies, one size does not fit all. It is important to be mindful of what works based on your particular style, interests, likes, and needs.

Physiological Needs: Resilience as the Foundation of Survival

Physiological needs—food, water, sleep, and physical health—form the foundation of Maslow's hierarchy. When these essentials are disrupted by stress, the resulting exhaustion and imbalance can hinder progress. Resilience ensures individuals maintain these needs even in difficult times.

Example of Challenges:

A caregiver juggling long work hours and family obligations might skip meals or sacrifice sleep. Without resilience, their physical health and emotional stability could decline, affecting their ability to care for others.

Potential Resilience Strategies:

1. Prioritize Sleep: Set consistent sleep schedules to restore energy and support emotional regulation.
2. Maintain Balanced Nutrition: Prepare regular meals and stay hydrated to stabilize energy levels and build physical resilience.

Safety Needs: Resilience as a Shield Against Instability

Safety needs, encompassing physical security, emotional stability, and financial reliability, become critical during high-stress periods. When unmet, they foster anxiety and make higher-level pursuits seem unattainable. Resilience provides the coping mechanisms needed to create stability amidst uncertainty.

Example of Challenges:

A family facing job loss may struggle to manage bills and emotional tensions. Without resilience, stress can escalate into conflict and instability.

Potential Resilience Strategies:

1. Prioritize Open Communication: Encourage honest and respectful conversations among family members about challenges, emotions, and possible solutions.
2. Focus on Problem-Solving: Break larger challenges into smaller, manageable tasks. Identify specific actions the family can take to address immediate concerns, such as budgeting, seeking assistance programs, or exploring new employment opportunities.

Love and Belonging: Resilience as a Bridge to Connection

Relationships are essential for emotional resilience. Maslow's love and belonging level highlights the importance of social connections to reduce stress and foster encouragement. Without resilience, feelings of isolation can hinder personal well-being.

Example of Challenges:

A remote worker struggling with loneliness might neglect relationships, leading to feelings of disconnection. Resilience empowers them to nurture social bonds even under stress.

Potential Resilience Strategies:

1. Lean on Social Support: Seek encouragement from trusted friends or family, which reinforces emotional stability and belonging.
2. Strengthen Empathy: Actively listen and show care in relationships, fostering gratitude and mutual understanding.

Esteem Needs: Resilience as a Catalyst for Confidence

Esteem needs include self-worth and recognition. When unmet, individuals may feel inadequate or lose motivation. Resilience allows them to maintain confidence and seek growth despite external pressures.

Example of Challenges:

A student struggling with academic setbacks may feel discouraged and question their abilities. Resilience enables them to reframe challenges as opportunities for growth.

Potential Resilience Strategies:

1. Celebrate Achievements: Acknowledge small victories to inspire hope and reinforce confidence.

2. Practice Positive Self-Talk: Replace self-doubt with constructive affirmations, fostering emotional balance and perseverance.

Self-Actualization: Resilience as a Path to Growth

At the top of Maslow's hierarchy, self-actualization represents personal growth and fulfillment. High-stress situations can stall progress here by creating overwhelm or disconnecting individuals from their goals. Resilience helps individuals align their actions with values, enabling them to pursue meaningful growth.

Example of Challenges:

An artist balancing financial stress with creative goals may feel pulled away from their purpose. Resilience empowers them to manage stress and stay committed to their aspirations.

Potential Resilience Strategies:

1. Engage in Mindfulness Practices: Use meditation or journaling to enhance self-awareness and emotional clarity which is key for self-actualization.

2. Align Actions With Values: Pursue activities that bring purpose and joy, building meaning and fulfillment.

Tying It All Together: Resilience as the Framework for Well-Being

Maslow's hierarchy provides a roadmap for meeting human needs. The Mason Resilience Model offers tools to address these needs effectively at each level with intentional strategies for individuals to strengthen their ability to regulate emotions and achieve personal growth. This integration ensures a balanced foundation for navigating life's complexities, fostering a fulfilling and resilient life. Resilience is the thread that connects physical, emotional, and social well-being, ensuring individuals adapt, recover, and grow despite challenges.

Resilience serves as both the framework and the practice for navigating life's challenges. Just as Maslow's hierarchy and the Mason Resilience Model highlight the importance of addressing human needs to foster growth and well-being, the analogy of surfing, which I will explain more in the next section, reminds us that resilience is an active, adaptive process. It's about equipping ourselves with the tools to face life's inevitable waves, balancing intentional strategies with emotional regulation. Together, these concepts underscore the transformative power of resilience—not as a static trait but as an ongoing skill set that enables us to stay grounded while moving forward.

Let's now explore how mastering the art of "surfing" life's waves helps us integrate resilience into every facet of our well-being.

You Can't Stop the Waves, But You Can Learn to Surf

Life's challenges often come at us like waves—some gentle and manageable, others towering and threatening to knock us completely off balance. These waves, whether they're stressors, unexpected events, or periods of uncertainty, are unavoidable. They're part of the natural rhythm of existence, ebbing and flowing with a force we cannot control. The key isn't about stopping the waves—that's impossible—but about learning how to surf. Surfing is more than just staying afloat; it's a skill—one that requires balance, adaptability, and perseverance.

Imagine standing at the shore, watching wave after wave approach. You can't turn back the tide, nor can you wish it away. At that moment, you have two choices: Resist the inevitable, dig your heels into the sand, and risk being swept under—or adapt, learn to balance yourself and move forward, riding each wave as it comes. Resilience becomes your surfboard, the tool that allows you to navigate the uncertainties of life with strength and confidence. It doesn't make the waves disappear, but it ensures they don't overwhelm you.

Consider a single parent juggling a demanding job while raising children and facing an unexpected financial strain. The wave of stress might feel like it's pulling them under. Without resilience, they could become stuck in feelings of helplessness and exhaustion. Instead, by adapting—seeking childcare support, restructuring their budget, and leaning on a trusted support system—they learn to ride the wave rather than being consumed by it. It's not easy, but each small act of resilience helps them stay afloat.

Now picture a college student grappling with academic setbacks, questioning their abilities after a series of low grades. The initial reaction might be to feel discouraged, standing frozen at the shore as the waves of self-doubt crash over them. But resilience offers another path. By reframing the challenges as opportunities for growth, seeking guidance from a mentor, and building better study habits, they begin to regain their balance. They learn to use the wave as momentum to propel them forward rather than letting it drag them down.

Even in professional life, the metaphor holds. Imagine a team leader or entrepreneur facing a significant project failure. The wave of disappointment and pressure to rebuild can be paralyzing. Yet, by focusing on the lessons learned, recalibrating their approach, and fostering open communication within the team, they use the setback as an opportunity to innovate and rebuild trust.

Surfing life's waves isn't about avoiding challenges or pretending they don't exist. It's about cultivating the skills to meet them head-on, to adapt, and to persevere even when the waters seem impossibly rough. The more waves we face, the better we become at maintaining our balance and moving forward. Each wave conquered, no matter how daunting, strengthens our ability to weather the next.

Whether it's a career shift, a personal loss, a health scare, or an unexpected change, every wave presents a chance to grow. Surfing these waves teaches us how to live with purpose and determination, embracing the ebbs and flows of life rather than fearing them. In the end, it's not the size of the wave that defines us but how we choose to ride it.

As we reflect on the metaphor of surfing life's waves, it's clear that resilience is not just a skill but a mindset—a way of approaching challenges with adaptability, strength, and intention. To deepen your understanding and apply these concepts to your own life, take a moment to explore the reflection questions that follow. These prompts are designed to help you think critically, evaluate your experiences, and take actionable steps toward building resilience and thriving amidst life's inevitable waves.

Let's dive in and begin this journey of self-discovery and growth.

Reflection

Prioritizing Physical, Emotional, and Mental Health

Resilience is built through intentional effort, self-awareness, and the ability to adapt to life's challenges. Prioritizing physical, emotional, and mental health is essential for maintaining balance and thriving, especially during high-stress situations. Take out your journal, settle into stillness, and embrace this opportunity to connect with yourself. This activity is designed to guide you in exploring your habits, thought patterns, and responses to challenges. By reflecting on how you address your well-being and identifying areas for growth, you can develop actionable strategies to strengthen your resilience and create a healthier, more balanced life.

Use these prompts to think deeply, analyze your current practices, and commit to meaningful changes that support your overall well-being. This is your opportunity to connect with what truly sustains you and take intentional steps toward living with clarity, purpose, and strength.

Think (Understanding & Awareness)

Consider these questions to explore your current understanding:

1. What does resilience mean to you, and how does it show up in your daily life?
2. How do you currently prioritize your physical, emotional, and mental health?
3. What are the "waves" in your life right now that feel most challenging to navigate?
4. In what ways do you typically respond to unexpected stressors or changes?
5. How do you recognize when your foundational needs (like sleep, nutrition, or safety) are not being met?

Evaluate (Analyzing & Reflecting)

Take time to analyze and reflect on your emotional habits and patterns:

1. Reflect on a recent high-stress situation. How did you handle it? What worked, and what could you improve?
2. When was there a time when you successfully rode the "waves" of life? What skills or resources helped you stay afloat?

3. What role do social support and relationships play in helping you manage challenges?

4. Think about a time when you neglected self-care. How did it impact your overall well-being and resilience?

5. How have your values or priorities influenced the way you approach self-care and emotional regulation?

Act (Implementation & Practice)

Turn your reflections into action with these practical steps:

1. What is one small change you can make this week to improve your physical health (e.g., better sleep, more movement)?

2. How can you incorporate mindfulness or reflection into your daily routine to enhance emotional clarity?

3. What is one strategy you can adopt to better manage high-stress situations in the future?

4. Who in your support system can you lean on for encouragement or advice? How will you reach out to them?

5. What specific action can you take to reframe a current challenge as an opportunity for growth?

As we reflect on the importance of prioritizing physical, emotional, and mental health, it's clear that maintaining balance and resilience is essential in navigating life's challenges. Understanding the connection between self-awareness and well-being equips us to handle stress, but putting this knowledge into practice is where true growth happens. To help you stay grounded in the face of uncertainty, we now turn to a practical tool designed to guide you back to the present moment. The 5-4-3-2-1 Grounding Exercise provides a simple yet effective way to center yourself, calm your mind, and reconnect with the world around you.

Let's explore how you can use this method to build strength and clarity when life feels overwhelming.

Activity

5-4-3-2-1 Grounding Exercise

In moments of stress or anxiety, it's easy to lose connection with the present, leaving us caught up in worry or fear. Life can sometimes feel overwhelming, like a relentless wave threatening to pull us under. This adaptation of Betty Erickson's 5-4-3-2-1 Grounding Exercise is a simple yet transformative tool that helps you find calm amidst the chaos by reconnecting with your surroundings.

This exercise works by engaging your five senses—sight, touch, hearing, smell, and taste—to anchor yourself firmly in the present moment. Scientifically, grounding techniques like this interrupt anxious thought patterns and help regulate the nervous system, shifting your focus away from the overwhelming and into what is tangible and manageable. By activating different sensory pathways, you redirect attention from spiraling emotions to the stability of the now, which fosters a sense of control and clarity.

Think of this practice as your mental surfboard, keeping you steady when life's waves seem too strong. Whether you're managing daily stress or navigating a crisis, the 5-4-3-2-1 method offers a reliable way to center yourself. Use this worksheet as a practical guide to implement this technique whenever the need arises—whether at home, work, or anywhere in between. Take a deep breath, trust the process, and let's dive into grounding with purpose and resilience.

Step 1: Identify Five Things You Can See

Look around you. Write down five things you can see. Be specific (e.g., "the blue vase on the shelf").

1. ______________________________
2. ______________________________
3. ______________________________
4. ______________________________
5. ______________________________

Step 2: Notice Four Things You Can Touch

Pay attention to textures and temperatures. Write down four things you can touch and describe their qualities.

1. ______________________________
2. ______________________________
3. ______________________________
4. ______________________________

Step 3: Listen for Three Sounds You Can Hear

Close your eyes if it helps. Write down three sounds you notice around you.

1. ______________________________

2. ______________________________

3. ______________________________

Step 4: Identify Two Things You Can Smell

Take a moment to focus on your sense of smell. Write down two scents you notice or imagine.

1. ______________________________

2. ______________________________

Step 5: Focus on One Thing You Can Taste

If you can, take a sip or a bite of something. Write down one thing you taste and describe it.

1. ______________________________

Reflection

How did this exercise make you feel?

____

____

____

____

____

Ending for Chapter 5: Staying Grounded in Chaos With Self-Care

As we conclude this chapter, let's reflect on the importance of cultivating resilience through self-care. Life's inevitable waves—whether they come as moments of stress, uncertainty, or significant change—challenge us in ways that can feel overwhelming. Yet, as we've explored, resilience is not about avoiding these waves but about learning how to ride them with balance, strength, and intention.

Through the lessons of Maslow's Hierarchy of Needs, the personal stories of triumph over chaos, and the practical strategies for maintaining physical, emotional, and mental health, we've seen how resilience is built one step at a time. It begins with small, intentional acts—getting enough rest, leaning on a support system, celebrating achievements, and anchoring ourselves in the present moment. These actions may seem simple, but their cumulative impact creates a strong foundation that enables us to persevere.

The 5-4-3-2-1 Grounding Exercise, introduced at the close of this chapter, is one such tool—an accessible method to pause, reflect, and regain clarity when the waves of life feel overwhelming. This practice exemplifies how grounding ourselves in the present can bring immediate relief and long-term strength.

As we move forward, remember that self-care is not selfish—it is the lifeline that allows you to show up fully for yourself and others. Resilience isn't a trait we're born with; it's a skill we develop through reflection, action, and mindfulness. Whether navigating a stormy sea or a calm horizon, the lessons of this chapter remind us that staying grounded is the key to thriving amidst chaos.

In the next chapter, we'll delve into another vital aspect of well-being: unlocking the transformative power of empathy. By understanding and embracing empathy as a superpower, we'll explore how it fosters deeper connections, strengthens relationships, and enhances both personal and professional growth. Together, let's continue building the mindset and skills that lead to a more meaningful, compassionate, and resilient life.

This book is meant to meet you where you are, so feel free to proceed to the next chapter or skip to the chapter that feels most relevant to you right now.

Chapter 6

Empathy as Your Superpower

- PRACTICING THE LUV MODEL ACROSS SCENARIOS
- REFLECTION: PRACTICING EMPATHY
- ACTIVITY: EMPATHY BINGO

6

Empathy As Your Superpower

"We must support each other and empathize with each other because each of us is more alike than we are unalike."
—Dr. Maya Angelou

Pause for a minute. When was the last time you truly felt seen or heard by someone? How often do you take a moment to step into someone else's shoes and consider their perspective? Those moments of genuine empathy can transform not just how we feel but how we connect with others.

Empathy is not just a concept; it's a skill that requires practice and intention to truly transform relationships and resolve conflicts. While the idea of walking in someone else's shoes is often easier said than done, it is through these deliberate efforts that we break down barriers and build meaningful connections.

Maya Angelou's words serve as a guiding principle of this chapter, reminding us that despite our differences, we share common threads of humanity. Empathy is the bridge that connects us, allowing us to understand, support, and care for one another.

In the pages ahead, I'll share a personal story that illustrates how empathy can transform even the most difficult dynamics into opportunities for trust, growth, and mutual respect. Together, we'll explore empathy's power to enhance both personal and professional relationships, promoting unity and understanding.

Empathy in Action: Transforming Conflict into Connection

In my time as a human resource (HR) professional, I encountered a division manager who had a reputation for being notoriously difficult. He had cycled through several HR partners before me, each relationship fraught with conflict, mistrust, and inefficiency. This manager was responsible for a large sector, a role inherently challenging and complex. Despite his critical position, his relationships with HR had been so strained that they were essentially nonfunctional.

One of his previous HR professionals shared a telling experience. She accompanied the division manager and another colleague to a meeting. In her words, he never looked at her, spoke to her, or even acknowledged her presence. She felt invisible, as though she were a ghost in the room. His perception of HR as a mere function rather than a strategic business partner had calcified over years of frustration and mistrust.

When I was assigned to be his HR professional, I braced for the same resistance. At first, his behavior toward me mirrored his past patterns: unresponsive, dismissive, and, at times, outright disrespectful. Instead of taking it personally, I decided to pause and approach the situation with curiosity. His behavior wasn't about me; it was a reflection of his own experiences and pain points.

I started asking questions, piecing together the history that shaped his perspective on HR. I learned that years ago, a previous HR professional had betrayed his trust in a professional context, leaving him disillusioned and guarded. That moment of insight fueled my empathy. I could see how his actions were rooted in hurt, and I became determined to rebuild his trust and show him a different side of the HR function.

For the next year, I leaned into empathy. Every interaction with him was intentional, centered on collaboration, kindness, and grace. I didn't let his initial resistance deter me. Instead, I focused on walking in his shoes—seeing the challenges he faced, the frustrations he carried, and the reasons behind his guarded demeanor. Slowly but surely, trust began to take root.

Then came the moment I knew our relationship had transformed. One day, he looked at me and said, "You know what? I've never liked HR people, but I love you as my HR partner." I was speechless! That simple statement carried immense weight. It was proof that empathy, patience, and consistent effort had broken through his walls.

This experience taught me that empathy isn't just about understanding someone else's perspective—it's about showing them grace and offering a safe space for healing and growth. By choosing to see his humanity beyond his behavior, I was able to change the dynamic of our partnership, repair his trust in HR, and pave the way for better collaboration.

What has the power to turn conflict into connection, mistrust into understanding, and resistance into partnership? Empathy has the power to create these transformative outcomes, fostering stronger relationships and collaboration. In this case, it not only transformed our working relationship but also reshaped his view of an entire profession. And for me, it reaffirmed the truth that walking in someone else's shoes can lead to outcomes that might once have seemed impossible.

Empathy has also been instrumental in making me a better coach. In my coaching practice, I've found that empathy is not just an important tool—it is the foundation for creating meaningful and effective client relationships. By deeply listening and understanding the unique challenges my clients face, I am able to meet them where they are, without judgment or preconceived notions. This connection allows me to create a safe space where clients feel seen and heard, which is often the catalyst they need to open up, reflect, and embrace growth.

For example, I've worked with clients who felt stuck in their careers or overwhelmed by personal obstacles. By leaning into empathy, I've been able to help them unpack their frustrations and fears, partnering with them as they find actionable solutions that align with their goals. Empathy allows me to look beyond the surface and understand the deeper emotions driving their decisions, which ultimately fosters trust and enables transformative progress. This skill, honed through experiences like my work with the difficult division manager, has shaped my approach to coaching and reinforced the power of seeing the world through another person's perspective.

In its truest form, the ability to understand and share another's perspective is a superpower that transcends roles and contexts, transforming potential conflict into collaboration and resistance into trust. Whether in a professional setting like HR, as a coach fostering growth, or in any relationship, empathy serves as the cornerstone for meaningful connection and progress. It requires us to slow down, listen deeply, and approach each interaction with curiosity and grace. Even the smallest acts of understanding and validation can create ripples of change, fostering an environment where everyone feels valued, heard, and supported.

Let's dive deeper into how we can harness this superpower in our own lives through practical tools and real-world applications.

Empathy in Action: Practicing the LUV Model Across Scenarios

The power of empathy goes beyond being just a skill—it's a transformative strength that deepens relationships and fosters genuine connections. It allows us to bridge divides, support others in their struggles, and create meaningful bonds in both personal and professional settings. Empathy empowers us to truly see and hear others, ensuring they feel valued and understood. The common practitioner tool, the LUV model—Listen, Understand, Validate—is a framework for harnessing this superpower, turning moments of connection into opportunities for trust, collaboration, and healing.

In her concept analysis, Theresa Wiseman (1996) identifies four defining attributes of empathy: seeing the world as others see it, being non-judgmental, understanding another's feelings, and communicating this understanding. Furthermore, as Brené Brown (2018) emphasizes, empathy is about connecting with others through shared humanity, not about offering solutions or minimizing feelings.

These principles align seamlessly with the LUV model, making it a powerful tool for putting empathy into action. Whether you're a nurse comforting a patient, a manager addressing an overwhelmed employee, or a friend consoling a loved one, empathy, when wielded as a superpower, has the potential to transform lives.

In this section, we explore how empathy sounds in practice across various scenarios. These examples show how the LUV model can be applied in different roles, turning understanding into action. Whether in moments of joy or hardship, empathy's superpower lies in its ability to create trust, foster resilience, and strengthen relationships.

A Nurse: Supporting a Worried Patient

Scenario: A patient awaiting test results expresses fear about their health.

- **Listen:** "I hear that you're feeling anxious about the results. Thank you for sharing that with me."
- **Understand:** "It's completely natural to feel worried when you're facing uncertainty about your health."
- **Validate:** "Anyone in your position would feel the same way. I'm here to support you through this."

Why It's a Superpower:

Empathy allows the nurse to ease the patient's anxiety, fostering trust and creating a sense of safety during a vulnerable moment.

A Life Coach: Encouraging a Client Facing a Career Change

Scenario: A client feels stuck and unsure about transitioning to a new career path.

- **Listen**: "You're saying you feel torn between excitement and fear about making this career move."
- **Understand**: "That's a big decision, and it makes sense that you're feeling a mix of emotions."
- **Validate**: "It's okay to feel uncertain—this is a major change, and those feelings are completely normal."

Why It's a Superpower:

The coach empowers the client to explore their emotions and take actionable steps, transforming fear into motivation.

A Sports Coach: Motivating an Athlete After a Tough Loss

Scenario: An athlete is discouraged after losing an important game.

- **Listen**: "I can see how disappointed you are about the loss. You gave it your all."
- **Understand**: "It's frustrating to work so hard and not get the outcome you hoped for."
- **Validate**: "Your effort and determination were incredible—this loss doesn't define your abilities or your potential."

Why It's a Superpower:

Empathy helps the athlete refocus and build resilience, turning a setback into an opportunity for growth.

A Manager: Addressing an Overwhelmed Employee

Scenario: An employee shares that they are feeling overwhelmed by their workload.

- **Listen**: "Thank you for letting me know how you're feeling. It's important that we address this."
- **Understand**: "Managing this workload sounds overwhelming—I can understand why it feels like too much."
- **Validate**: "I hear you. It's not easy to juggle everything, and I want to work with you to find a better balance."

Why It's a Superpower:

Empathy creates an open and supportive work environment, enabling the employee to feel seen and valued.

A Coworker: Supporting a Colleague Facing a Personal Loss

Scenario:A coworker shares that they've lost a loved one.

- **Listen:** "I'm so sorry for your loss. Thank you for sharing this with me."
- **Understand:** "I can't imagine how hard this is for you. Losing someone you love is incredibly painful."
- **Validate:** "It's okay to grieve and take the time you need. Your feelings are completely valid, and I'm here if you need anything."

Why It's a Superpower:

Empathy strengthens workplace relationships, creating a culture of support and understanding.

A Mother: Calming a Frustrated Child

Scenario: A child is upset because they feel left out at school.

- **Listen:** "I hear you saying you felt left out when your friends didn't include you today."
- **Understand:** "That must have felt really lonely and unfair—it's hard when friends don't act the way we hope they will."
- **Validate:** "It's okay to feel sad about this. I get where you are coming from, and I'm proud of you for sharing them with me."

Why It's a Superpower:

Empathy helps the child feel understood and supported, teaching emotional resilience and self-expression.

Why Empathy as a Superpower Matters

In each of these scenarios, empathy transforms ordinary interactions into moments of connection, healing, and collaboration. The LUV model offers a practical roadmap for applying empathy, ensuring that others feel seen, heard, and validated. Empathy isn't about fixing someone's problems—it's about walking alongside them, offering understanding and support.

Bridging the gap between intention and connection, empathy enables us to build relationships grounded in understanding and trust. The scenarios I explored highlight how empathy, when applied through the LUV model, can transform interactions and foster a sense of belonging. Yet, empathy goes beyond simply listening or validating—it challenges us to step into another's perspective, to see the world as they see it.

This brings us to the concept of "walking in their shoes," a powerful metaphor for empathy in action. By imagining what it's like to experience life from someone else's point of view, we deepen our ability to connect and communicate effectively. Let's delve into what it truly means to borrow someone else's shoes for a journey of empathy and understanding.

Walking in Their Shoes: A Journey of Empathy

What does it truly mean to "walk in someone else's shoes," as empathy is often described? Picture borrowing someone else's shoes for a journey. The shoes might feel unfamiliar—too tight, too loose, or just different from what you're used to. Yet, as you walk, you begin to experience the world as they do, encountering the same terrain, challenges, and emotions. Empathy works in much the same way. It's not just about imagining someone's experiences but stepping into their perspective, feeling their joys, struggles, and fears, and understanding how those emotions shape their actions and choices.

The metaphor of "if the shoe fits, wear it" adds another layer of meaning to empathy. It reminds us that our own perspective isn't universal; what fits for one person may not work for another. Empathy requires not only recognizing differences but also adapting our approach to align with someone else's reality. It's about meeting people where they are, not where we think they should be.

The Value of Empathy in Practice

Walking in someone else's shoes isn't about perfect understanding—it's about being willing to try. Empathy enables us to approach differences not as barriers but as opportunities for deeper connection. It encourages us to set aside assumptions, ask questions, and embrace the discomfort of learning something new. This practice not only enriches our interactions but also strengthens our ability to navigate an interconnected world.

Far from being just a concept, empathy is a practice that demands active effort and thoughtful self-reflection. But understanding the value of empathy is only the first step—putting it into action is where transformation happens. To truly harness empathy as a superpower, we must reflect on how we approach it in our daily lives and consider tangible ways to improve. This next section offers an opportunity to pause, think critically, and develop strategies for practicing empathy more intentionally.

Reflection

Practicing Empathy

A skill that grows with practice, self-awareness, and intentional effort, empathy has the power to transform relationships and deepen understanding. While understanding empathy in theory is important, applying it in our daily lives is what brings its true power to light. Take some paper, settle into a soothing atmosphere, and give yourself permission to reflect deeply. This reflection and application activity is designed to help you deepen your understanding of empathy, evaluate your current habits, and identify practical ways to enhance this essential skill.

By reflecting on your thoughts, actions, and interactions, you can uncover opportunities for growth and recognize the impact empathy has on your relationships—both personal and professional. Whether it's through active listening, creating safe spaces for others to share, or breaking down barriers to understanding, these exercises will guide you toward a more empathetic approach to life. Take your time with these questions and activities. They are not just tools for self-reflection but also pathways to creating stronger, more meaningful connections with those around you.

Think (Understanding & Awareness)

Consider these questions to explore your current understanding:

1. How do you define empathy, and why is it important?
2. What does "walking in someone else's shoes" mean to you?
3. How does empathy influence your personal and professional relationships?
4. What barriers prevent you from fully understanding others' perspectives?
5. How do you currently demonstrate empathy in your daily interactions?

Evaluate (Analyzing & Reflecting)

Take time to analyze and reflect on your emotional habits and patterns:

1. Reflect on a moment when empathy transformed a relationship or situation.
2. How do you balance showing empathy while maintaining your own boundaries?
3. What patterns do you notice in how you listen to others?

4. How has receiving empathy from others impacted you?
5. In what ways can you grow your ability to see the world from others' perspectives?

Act (Implementation & Practice)

Turn your reflections into action with these practical steps:

1. What is one active listening technique you'll practice this week?
2. How can you show empathy to someone you disagree with?
3. What step will you take to build trust in a challenging relationship?
4. How can you create space for someone to share their feelings without judgment?
5. What daily habit will help you practice empathy more consistently?

Practicing empathy exercises introduces the importance of deliberate, thoughtful actions to deepen our understanding of others and enhance our ability to connect. These exercises encourage us to reflect on how empathy shapes our interactions and identifies areas for growth.

To put empathy into practice in a fun and engaging way, let's dive into Empathy Bingo. This activity challenges you to complete specific empathy-driven actions throughout the week, turning reflection into action and strengthening your empathy muscles one square at a time.

B	I	N	G	O
Used the LUV model (Listen, Understand, Validate)	Recognized non-verbal cues during a conversation	Asked an open-ended question	Acknowledged someone's strengths during a conversation	Apologized sincerely to someone
Encouraged someone to share more about their feelings or thoughts	Expressed understanding when someone made a mistake	Acknowledged someone's perspective without judgment	Listened without interrupting	Respected someone's need for space or silence
Let someone vent without trying to fix their problem	Avoided making assumptions about someone's intentions	FREE SPACE!	Reframed a conflict by considering the other person's viewpoint	Practiced active listening during a conversation
Checked in on someone going through a tough time	Validated someone's emotions	Expressed curiosity about someone's opinion without inserting your own	Paused to reflect before responding to someone's emotions	Gave someone the benefit of the doubt in a disagreement
Expressed gratitude for someone's support	Asked someone how they're doing and really listened to their response	Thanked someone for sharing their feelings or perspective	Took a moment to empathize with someone's frustration or stress	Made eye contact and gave full attention while someone spoke

Activity

Empathy Bingo

More than just understanding others, empathy is about transforming that understanding into meaningful action. The Empathy Bingo Worksheet challenges you to engage in meaningful, empathy-driven actions throughout the week. Each square represents a simple yet impactful way to practice empathy, whether it's through listening actively, validating emotions, or showing gratitude.

As you complete the actions and record them on this worksheet, you'll discover opportunities to deepen your connections, navigate challenges with compassion, and build stronger relationships. Whether you complete one row, column, diagonal, or even the entire card, this activity is designed to make empathy an intentional and natural part of your daily interactions.

At the end of the week, reflect on your experiences using the guided questions below. What actions felt most natural? Which ones challenged you? Through this practice, you'll not only enhance your empathy but also uncover insights about yourself and your relationships.

Reflection Questions:

1. Which empathy-driven actions felt the most impactful this week, and why?

   ___

   ___

   ___

2. Were there any actions that felt challenging to complete? What made them difficult?

   ___

   ___

   ___

3. How do you think practicing these actions has influenced your relationships or interactions?

   ___

   ___

   ___

4. Which empathy-driven actions do you want to incorporate into your daily life moving forward?

____

____

____

Ending for Chapter 6: Empathy as Your Superpower

As we close Chapter 6, it's clear that empathy's true value lies in its application—in moments of listening, understanding, and validating those around us. From practicing the LUV model to engaging in activities like Empathy Bingo, we have explored how empathy bridges gaps, fosters trust, and strengthens relationships in personal and professional settings.

As you reflect on the stories, tools, and activities in this chapter, think about how empathy can become a more intentional part of your life. Whether by walking in someone else's shoes, creating space for others to share their feelings, or simply being present in your daily interactions, each small act of empathy has the potential to create ripples of change.

The practice of empathy is a journey, not a destination. By committing to continuous practice, self-awareness, and reflection, you can harness this superpower to navigate challenges, resolve conflicts, and build a more compassionate world—one connection at a time.

In the next chapter, we will explore the transformative power of positive emotions and their role in shaping our energy, mindset, and relationships. Get ready to dive into positivity and discover practical strategies to cultivate joy, gratitude, and resilience in your daily life.

Let's harness the energy of positive emotions to thrive and uplift ourselves and those around us!

Or you can choose to navigate to a chapter that aligns with your current needs.

Chapter 7

The Energy of Positive Emotions

- EMBRACING POSITIVE EMOTIONS IN THE MIDST OF CHAOS
- REFLECTION: THE ENERGY OF POSITIVE EMOTIONS
- ACTIVITY: OPEN WINDOW GRATITUDE JOURNAL

7

The Energy of Positive Emotions

"Staying positive doesn't mean you have to be happy all the time.
It means that even on hard days you know that there are
better ones coming."
—Anonymous

Have you ever faced a moment when staying hopeful felt nearly impossible? Maybe it was a difficult day, a missed opportunity, or a time when life seemed to throw challenge after challenge your way. How did you find the strength to keep going, or what held you back from believing in brighter days?

Staying positive doesn't mean ignoring the hard days or forcing happiness when it feels out of reach. Instead, it's about believing in the possibility of better days ahead—a mindset that gives us strength during life's most challenging moments. This idea is at the heart of positive emotions and their transformative power. Positivity isn't about erasing struggles; it's about choosing hope, embracing gratitude, and finding joy in the small moments, even amidst difficulty.

In Chapter 7, we'll explore how the energy of positive emotions can shift our perspectives, foster resilience, and enhance our well-being. This quote serves as a reminder that positivity is a practice, not perfection. It's about leaning into the belief that hard times are temporary and that brighter days are always on the horizon. By cultivating positive emotions, we don't just weather life's storms; we discover the strength to grow through them.

The energy of positive emotions lies in their ability to transform even the most challenging experiences into opportunities for growth and discovery. While moments of disappointment or setback can feel overwhelming, they often carry hidden lessons or gems and the potential for redirection toward something even greater.

As we explore the connection between positivity and resilience, my personal journey serves as a testament to the power of hope and perspective. What began as a career disappointment, evolved into a profound moment of gratitude and purpose, demonstrating that the detours in life can lead to destinations we never expected but were always meant to reach.

The Opportunity in Disappointment: Finding Purpose in Life's Detours

In May of 2005, I was on the cusp of a significant career milestone within my organization. I had accepted a promotion to human resource manager, a role I had worked tirelessly to earn. I began planning my relocation, brimming with excitement and anticipation for this next chapter. I had already told my family and friends, proudly sharing the news of this achievement. I had given notice at my apartment, mentally preparing for the move and everything it would bring.

Then, just weeks later, I received unexpected news—our corporate office had decided to franchise out all locations in Louisiana. This decision rendered the role of human resource manager unnecessary, and just like that, my promotion was gone. My mind raced with questions: *What? What will I do now? How will I explain this to everyone I've already told? What about the plans I so carefully made?* I felt blindsided, disappointed, and unsure of what the future held.

At that moment, I chose to anchor myself in a belief that has guided me throughout my life: What is truly meant for me will never pass me by. This mindset allowed me to navigate the initial disappointment with a small sense of hope and trust in the unfolding of life. I couldn't have known then how this perspective would protect me in ways I would only come to understand months later.

On August 29, 2005, Hurricane Katrina made landfall, devastating New Orleans and the surrounding areas. The levee breach in the Lower Ninth Ward led to catastrophic flooding, forcing many residents into unimaginable hardship. As someone who grew up in Tampa, Florida—a place often spared the worst of hurricanes—I had become desensitized to the true dangers they posed. Had I relocated to Louisiana as planned, I would have likely underestimated the severity of the storm. The consequences of that miscalculation could have been life-altering.

Reflecting on this chain of events, I am struck by a profound sense of gratitude and humility. Losing the promotion I had so eagerly anticipated initially felt like a setback. But in hindsight, it was a redirection—a way to spare me from potentially devastating circumstances. This realization deepened my appreciation for the role that external factors, often beyond our control, play in shaping our paths.

The experience reinforced a crucial life lesson: Sometimes not getting what we want is a gift in disguise. It's an opportunity to rewrite the narrative, to trust that better days are ahead, and to find meaning even in moments of disappointment. This mindset aligns with the energy of positive emotions—hope, gratitude, and resilience—that can sustain us during challenging times.

Hurricane Katrina's devastating impact on the residents of New Orleans serves as a powerful reminder of humanity's incredible strength and resilience in the face of adversity. Their unwavering determination to rebuild and move forward inspires me to confront my own challenges with the same courage and perseverance. It also reinforces my commitment to embracing every opportunity with gratitude and to extending support to those in need whenever possible.

So, the lesson here is clear: Sometimes life's detours are blessings in disguise. They remind us that the things we don't get might save us or lead us to something even greater. Holding onto the belief that better days are coming—even when faced with uncertainty—infuses our lives with a sense of purpose and positivity that keeps us moving forward.

Positive emotions provide the foundation for resilience and well-being, offering a way to navigate life's ups and downs with strength and optimism. However, cultivating positivity in the midst of chaos, loss, or personal storms is far from easy. It requires us to confront our emotional realities while intentionally seeking moments of light. This dual approach—acknowledging our struggles while embracing positive emotions—helps us strike a balance that fosters growth and healing.

Let's explore how we can "keep it real" by integrating positivity into our lives, even during life's most challenging moments.

The Science of Positive Psychology

Positive emotions lie at the heart of positive psychology, a field dedicated to exploring what makes life meaningful and how individuals and communities can thrive. Pioneered by psychologist Martin Seligman in the late 1990s, positive psychology focuses on fostering well-being, promoting resilience, and cultivating personal growth.

Central to this approach is understanding how positive emotions—like joy, gratitude, hope, and love—shape not just our mental and emotional health but also our physical well-being (Seligman, 2000).

Unlike traditional psychology, which often centers on diagnosing and treating mental illness, positive psychology shifts the focus to enhancing what makes life fulfilling. Barbara Fredrickson (2001) highlights the transformative role of positive emotions, emphasizing their ability to fuel personal growth, inspire creativity, and build resilience. These emotions are not fleeting moments of happiness; they are enduring forces that strengthen our ability to navigate challenges and embrace opportunities.

However, maintaining positive emotions isn't always easy, particularly during times of chaos or loss. Life's inevitable storms can make it feel impossible to hold on to positivity. This raises an important question: How can we cultivate positive emotions even in the midst of personal and collective challenges? To answer this, we must first understand the science behind our emotional responses and how to harness positivity as a tool for resilience and growth.

Keeping It Real: Embracing Positive Emotions in the Midst of Chaos

Let's be honest—cultivating positive emotions in the middle of chaos, loss, or personal storms can feel like an impossible task. When life is overwhelming, fear, frustration, or sadness often take center stage. This isn't a personal failure—it's a reflection of our human design. Our brains are wired for survival, not immediate positivity, which explains why negative emotions tend to dominate during stressful times.

At the core of this response is the amygdala, a small almond-shaped structure in the brain responsible for processing fear and

other intense emotions. When we perceive a threat—whether it's a physical danger or the emotional weight of a loss—the amygdala activates the fight-or-flight response, prioritizing survival above all else (Goleman, 1995). While this mechanism is crucial for protecting us in moments of immediate danger, it can also make it difficult to access broader perspectives or tap into positive emotions. In these moments, anxiety, anger, or grief often cloud our ability to see the light ahead.

Navigating life's storms requires more than just a "think positive" mantra—it demands a delicate balance of honoring our negative emotions while actively seeking moments of light. By understanding the brain's survival mechanisms and learning to coexist with all of our emotions, we can cultivate resilience, even in the toughest circumstances. The next step is learning how to embrace positive emotions as a tool for healing and growth.

Feeling to Heal

Daniel Goleman's work on emotional intelligence (see also chapters 1, and 4) underscores that embracing positive emotions during difficult times doesn't mean denying or suppressing negative ones. It's not about pretending that everything is fine but about finding a balance. It's about believing you have both the will and the way to persevere. Negative emotions serve an essential purpose; they're like emotional check-engine lights, signaling that something needs attention and helping us process pain or recognizing when to seek support (Goleman, 1995). Ignoring these feelings or forcing positivity is like slapping a happy-face sticker over that warning light—it doesn't fix the problem and only makes it harder to move forward.

True emotional health involves acknowledging all emotions—both positive and negative—and using self-awareness to navigate them constructively. Positive emotions do not erase the pain of chaos or loss; instead, they serve as an anchor, offering moments of light amidst the darkness. Even small doses of positive emotions, like a fleeting moment of gratitude or a shared laugh over something silly, can foster resilience and remind us that better days will come (Fredrickson, 2001).

The Challenge of Positivity in the Storm

Finding positivity during life's most difficult moments can feel daunting. In these times, positive emotions may look different from the exuberant joy we associate with happiness. Instead, they might take the form of gratitude for a small act of kindness, pride in making it through another day, or hope that the storm will eventually pass. These emotions don't negate the pain of the moment; rather, they coexist with it, showing that it's possible to hold both struggle and strength at the same time.

This duality is where the power of positive emotions shines. By intentionally leaning into gratitude, hope, or love, we engage the brain's prefrontal cortex, which governs rational thought and emotional regulation. This allows us to reframe our narratives, focus on solutions, and find moments of connection or relief (Goleman, 1995). Positive emotions help quiet the amygdala's alarm bells, restoring balance to our emotional state and creating space for healing and growth.

Why It Matters

Maintaining positive emotions during chaos isn't about denying our humanity—it's about embracing it. While we may not have control over life's storms, we can control how we respond to them. Positive emotions provide the resilience needed to weather these challenges, reminding us that even in the darkest moments, light is still within reach (Fredrickson, 2001). By honoring all of our emotions—positive and negative alike—we cultivate emotional intelligence and strength that extend far beyond any single challenge, equipping us to navigate life with courage and grace.

As we navigate life's challenges, maintaining positive emotions becomes a powerful act of resilience. These emotions don't erase our struggles, but they create moments of clarity and balance, offering a way to endure and grow. Like a lifeline during chaos, they remind us that light exists even in the darkest corners.

To truly understand the impact of positive emotions, let's explore how they act as an open window in our lives—letting in fresh air and new perspectives when everything feels heavy and stagnant. Through this analogy, we'll uncover the transformative power of positivity to refresh our outlook and energize our journey forward.

An Open Window: The Power of Positive Emotions

Imagine being in a stuffy room—stale air, oppressive heat, and a feeling of confinement. Then, you crack open a window, and a cool breeze flows in. Suddenly, the atmosphere changes. You feel refreshed, lighter, and able to think more clearly. This is what positive emotions do for us, especially when life feels stagnant or overwhelming. They create space for renewal, allowing us to breathe, shift our perspective, and move forward.

Positive emotions act as that open window, offering relief from the mental and emotional heaviness that negative emotions can bring. They don't erase the challenges we face, but they bring in fresh energy and clarity, helping us to see situations in a new light. Whether it's the joy of reconnecting with an old friend, the gratitude sparked by an unexpected kindness, or the hope that tomorrow might be better than today, these emotions open the door to possibilities we may not have seen before.

The Fresh Air of Clarity

When positive emotions flow in, they break the cycle of ruminating on problems or getting stuck in unhelpful thought patterns. For example, experiencing gratitude can shift our focus from what we lack to what we have, providing a sense of abundance instead of scarcity. Hope can transform fear into motivation, helping us take steps forward even when the path isn't entirely clear.

Research in positive psychology supports this transformative effect. According to Barbara Fredrickson's Broaden-and-Build Theory (2001), positive emotions expand our awareness and encourage creative thinking. Like that open window, they allow us to "broaden" our perspectives, helping us to build resilience, nurture relationships, and solve problems with newfound energy.

A New Perspective Through the Window

Sometimes, when life feels particularly overwhelming, even a small positive emotion can act as that window, offering a glimpse of what lies beyond the walls we've built. For instance, in moments of chaos, simply pausing to appreciate something small—a beautiful sunset, a child's laughter, or the satisfaction of completing a task—can remind us that there's more to our lives than the immediate stressor.

This doesn't mean we ignore what's difficult. The window doesn't remove the room's stuffiness; it simply provides an alternative. Positive emotions coexist with negative ones, offering balance and perspective. They remind us that while pain and struggle are real, so are joy, connection, and hope.

Life's challenges can feel like they seal us in a room with no exit, but positive emotions remind us that we always have access to an open window. They bring fresh energy, clarity, and the perspective needed to navigate even the most difficult circumstances. By intentionally cultivating these emotions, we can turn moments of stagnation into opportunities for growth, connection, and renewal.

So, the next time life feels overwhelming, remember: The window is always there. All it takes is a little effort to open it and let the breeze of positive emotions shift the air around you. But sustaining this breeze requires more than recognition—it takes reflection and intentional practice.

The next section invites you to explore how positive emotions shape your resilience and daily life. Through reflection and action, you'll uncover insights to deepen your connection with positivity and make it a lasting source of growth and strength.

Let's open the window a little wider and let positivity guide the way forward.

Reflection

The Energy of Positive Emotions

Positive emotions are the energy that propels us forward, especially during life's most challenging moments. They don't erase difficulties, but they give us the strength to navigate them with resilience and hope. Like an open window letting in fresh air, positive emotions bring clarity, perspective, and renewal. However, cultivating these emotions requires intention, self-awareness, and a willingness to reflect on our experiences.

Grab your journal, choose a tranquil environment, and invite yourself into a moment of self-discovery. In this section, we'll dive into reflection questions designed to help you think deeply about how positive emotions shape your life, evaluate how they coexist with challenges, and take actionable steps to integrate them into your daily routines. These questions aren't just about intellectual understanding—they're about fostering growth, building emotional resilience, and unlocking the transformative power of positivity in your journey forward.

Think (Understanding & Awareness)

Consider these questions to explore your current understanding:

1. What does the phrase "staying positive" mean to you, and how does it influence your daily outlook?
2. How do you personally define positive emotions, and which ones resonate with you the most?
3. Reflect on the analogy of an open window. How do positive emotions create space for renewal in your life?
4. What role do positive emotions play in helping you navigate stressful or overwhelming situations?
5. How do negative emotions coexist with positive ones in your emotional experience?

Evaluate (Analyzing & Reflecting)

Take time to analyze and reflect on your emotional habits and patterns:

1. Think about a time when positive emotions helped you shift your perspective during a difficult moment. What changed for you?
2. How do you currently handle negative emotions when life feels chaotic or challenging?
3. What patterns do you notice in your ability to experience grati-

tude, hope, or joy during tough times?

4. Reflect on a specific moment of gratitude or joy. How did it affect your ability to handle adversity?
5. In what ways have you experienced the balance between honoring your negative emotions and intentionally cultivating positive ones?

Act (Implementation & Practice)

Turn your reflections into action with these practical steps:

1. What is one step you can take this week to intentionally cultivate positive emotions, even in small moments?
2. How can you use the concept of an open window to reframe a current challenge in your life?
3. What practical strategies will you adopt to acknowledge your negative emotions while leaning into positive ones?
4. How will you incorporate gratitude or other positive emotions into your daily routine to foster resilience?
5. What small action can you take today to open a window of positivity in your life or the life of someone else?

Reflection is the first step in understanding how positive emotions influence our lives, but putting those insights into action is where transformation happens. One of the simplest and most effective ways to cultivate positive emotions is through practicing gratitude. By shifting our focus from what's lacking to what we have, gratitude helps us reframe challenges and strengthen our emotional resilience.

In the next section, we'll explore the power of keeping a gratitude journal—a practical tool to anchor positivity in your daily life. This activity offers a meaningful way to capture moments of joy, connection, and hope, no matter how small they may seem. Let's turn reflection into practice and discover the transformative energy of gratitude.

Activity

Open Window Gratitude Journal

Gratitude has the power to transform the way we view our lives, offering clarity and a renewed sense of purpose—just like opening a window in a stuffy room. The Open Window Gratitude Journal is designed to help you cultivate this positive energy intentionally. By focusing on the things you're grateful for each day, you'll begin to see how even small moments can have a profound impact on your mood, perspective, and overall well-being.

This journal isn't just about listing what you're thankful for—it's a space for deeper reflection. Over time, this practice will not only increase your awareness of the positive influences in your life but also help you navigate challenges with greater resilience and optimism. Here's a sample template to get you started with gratitude journaling. I recommend transferring it to a notebook and using it as a springboard for your daily reflections.

Use the template below to fill out the following columns.

- **Date:** *Write the current date at the start of each new entry.*
- **Gratitude Item:** *Enter one different thing you are grateful for each day. Use additional rows for more items if needed.*
- **Why I'm Grateful:** *For each item listed, provide a specific reason why you feel gratitude toward it.*

- **Positive Impact:** *Reflect on how each item has positively affected your day or your life.*
- **Emotional Reflection:** *Note any changes in your mood or emotional state after completing your gratitude entries.*

EXAMPLES				
	Gratitude Item	Why I'm Grateful	Positive Impact	Emotional Reflection
July 23, 2024	Support from my best friend.	Grateful for my friend's encouragement during a stressful project at work.	Helped me stay motivated and less overwhelmed.	Felt supported and less isolated, uplifted my mood significantly.
July 24, 2024	Completing a difficult task.	Grateful for finishing a challenging assignment ahead of schedule.	Boosted my confidence in my professional abilities.	Felt accomplished and proud of my diligence.
July 24, 2024	Sunny morning walk.	Grateful for the peaceful start to my day with a walk under the clear, blue sky.	Enhanced my mood and energy levels for the day.	Felt refreshed and connected to nature.
July 25, 2024	Enjoying a cup of coffee.	Grateful for the quiet moments in the morning enjoying my favorite coffee.	Gave me a sense of routine and comfort.	Felt calm and content, a perfect start to the day.

Weekly Highlights:

- At the end of the week, review your daily entries and note any themes or recurring items.
- Identify the top two things you were most grateful for throughout the week.

Reflection Questions:

- How has this week's gratitude practice affected your overall mood and outlook?
- What have you learned about what truly matters to you?

Date	**Gratitude Item** *(i.e., relationships, personal achievements, self-growth, nature, or simple pleasures)*	**Why I'm Grateful**	**Positive Impact**	**Emotional Reflection**

Next Week's Focus:

- Based on this week's reflections, set a goal or focus for the next week's gratitude entries. For example, focus more on people, self-growth, or experiences.

Tips for Effective Journaling:

- **Be Specific**: Instead of broad statements like "I'm grateful for my family," specify what about your family you're grateful for, such as "I'm grateful for my partner's support during a tough day."
- **Vary Your Focus**: Try to include different areas of your life in your gratitude entries, such as relationships, personal achievements, nature, or simple pleasures.
- **Reflect Deeply**: Take a moment to truly feel the gratitude as you write, which can enhance the emotional benefits of this practice.

Ending for Chapter 7: The Energy of Positive Emotions

Positive emotions are more than fleeting moments of joy—they are the foundation of resilience and growth, especially during life's most challenging times. They offer a perspective shift, a renewed sense of hope, and a way to navigate chaos with clarity and strength. Through cultivating gratitude, embracing small moments of joy, and balancing our emotional landscape, we learn that positivity isn't about perfection; it's about perseverance, practice, and trial and error.

As we open the window to positive emotions, we unlock a powerful tool for not just surviving but thriving. This chapter has explored how positivity energizes us, helps us reframe setbacks, and fuels resilience. It reminds us that even when the path is unclear, the light of hope, gratitude, and connection can guide us forward.

But, positivity alone isn't enough to sustain us. Beyond resilience lies the deeper question: What drives us? What gives our lives meaning? In the next chapter, we'll explore the transformative power of discovering your purpose and creating a life that feels fulfilling and intentional. Just as positive emotions open the window to possibility, meaning and purpose anchor us, giving our journey direction and clarity.

There's no set order to your self-discovery journey. Feel free to go to an alternative chapter that calls to you and feels most fitting for where you are.

Chapter 8

Purpose & Meaning in Life

- DEFINING PURPOSE AND MEANING
- REFLECTION: PURPOSE AND MEANING OF LIFE
- ACTIVITY: CELEBRATING YOUR LEGACY

8

Purpose & Meaning In Life

"The two most important days in your life are the day you are born and the day you find out why."

—Often attributed to Mark Twain, though of uncertain origin

Have you ever paused to ask yourself why you're here? What gives your life meaning beyond the daily routines and responsibilities? Is it the relationships you've built, the passions you pursue, or the impact you hope to leave behind? These are questions that may not have easy answers, but they sit at the heart of what it means to live a purposeful life.

Mark Twain's quote, "The two most important days in your life are the day you are born and the day you find out why," encapsulates the essence of purpose and meaning in life. Our birth marks the beginning of our existence, but it's the discovery of our "why" that gives that existence depth and significance. This "why" represents the unique combination of our passions, values, and contributions that make our lives fulfilling and impactful. Purpose and meaning often emerge in the most unexpected ways, like navigating a path that changes direction without warning. Twain encourages us to seek our "why," but the process is unique for everyone, defined by the challenges we face and the ways we grow. It's not solely about arriving at a destination—it's about the lessons we gather, the resilience we build, and the emotional intelligence we develop along the way.

Discovering your "why" isn't a single, dramatic epiphany—it's a continuous journey of self-discovery, shaped by understanding who you are and how you can make a difference. This journey, filled with twists, turns, and opportunities for growth, is what transforms life from mere existence to a truly meaningful experience. Purpose and meaning rarely appear all at once; instead, they gradually reveal themselves through our experiences, challenges, and moments of reflection. Twain's words remind us that finding our purpose adds richness to our lives and gives us something worth celebrating.

With that in mind, let's take a closer look at my early journey: a winding yellow brick road of detours, discoveries, and the eventual clarity that comes from embracing the unexpected much like the path envisioned by L. Frank Baum in *The Wonderful Wizard of Oz*.

My Journey: Finding Clarity on the Yellow Brick Road

I set off on my yellow brick road at 18 years old, bursting with ambition and optimism, only to discover that the road to purpose is rarely straight or smooth. This is the tale of my seven-year journey to discover my true passion and purpose in life. By age 25, I had uncovered what truly mattered to me—a blessing, I realize, to have found relatively early in life. But let's be real: discovering purpose isn't a race. Whether you stumble upon it in your 30s, 40s, 50s, or beyond, the journey is equally valuable. Purpose isn't some magical Emerald City you stumble into—it's something you reveal through living, learning, and navigating the twists, turns, and occasional tornadoes of life.

Off to See the Wizard: My Journey Begins

At 18, I was full of ambition, optimism, and a clear goal: to become Dr. Shirita the Psychologist. Like Baum's Dorothy stepping onto the yellow brick road, I was determined to reach my Emerald City. I enrolled at the University of South Florida, threw myself into psychology courses, and sought out mentors to guide me. The human mind fascinated me, and I dreamed of helping others understand themselves and overcome challenges. My path seemed set.

But as Dorothy learned, life rarely follows a straight road. Tornadoes of unexpected opportunities and challenges swept in, spinning me into unfamiliar territory and forcing me to grow in ways I hadn't anticipated. At the time, I couldn't have known that emotional intelligence and resilience would be the companions that helped me navigate the twists and turns of my yellow brick road.

Tornadoes and Pearl Slippers: Navigating the Unexpected

Like the tornado that carried Dorothy to Oz, life's upheavals often dropped me into new, uncharted territory. My journey wasn't a straight line—instead, it veered into unexpected industries and roles. I often worked 2-3 jobs simultaneously, juggling positions in education, psychology, and human resources. At times, I wondered if I resembled the stereotypical college student who changed majors every few months. Each job and pivot left me questioning: Am I still on the path to becoming Dr. Shirita the Psychologist?

One of the first tornadoes swept me into a business organization where I discovered skills like professionalism, business acumen, and public speaking. Yikes, I learned that I loved business! I thrived in leadership roles, sales, and business, but I constantly wrestled with the question: How will this help me achieve my dream? Each detour forced me to tap into emotional intelligence—the ability to manage my emotions and recognize the value in new experiences, even when they didn't align with my original plan.

The Lion, Tin Man, and Scarecrow: Finding Courage, Heart, and Wisdom

Throughout my journey, emotional intelligence and resilience showed up like Baum's Lion, Tin Man, and Scarecrow, guiding me through the challenges of self-discovery and meaning:

- The Lion taught me courage as I faced the uncertainty of stepping into new roles. Whether it was leading teams, transitioning to HR, or learning compliance, I leaned on resilience to push through the fear of the unknown.
- The Tin Man reminded me of the importance of heart. My work at the Francis House, supporting those impacted by HIV/AIDS, revealed the depth of my compassion. This emotionally intense experience taught me to honor my limits and focus on roles where I could make a meaningful impact without depleting myself.
- The Scarecrow encouraged me to value wisdom and adaptability. My pivots into HR, recruiting, and marketing expanded my skill set and taught me the power of learning from every experience, no matter how far it seemed from my original goal.

These character traits reminded me that emotional intelligence isn't just about understanding others—it's also about understanding myself. Resilience, meanwhile, gave me the strength to keep moving forward, even when the road seemed uncertain.

Finding Purpose in Detours

At 21, I hit a pivotal moment during my time at the Francis House. This emotionally challenging role tested my resilience and forced me to reevaluate my direction. While I loved helping others, I realized that I was at my best when I balanced my strengths with my emotional capacity. This clarity shifted my focus toward roles that aligned with my skills and values.

Similarly, my pivot to human resources introduced me to compliance, safety, coaching, and leadership development. While these roles seemed disconnected from psychology at first glance, they revealed common threads: fostering growth, creating structure, and empowering others. Each step added a tool to my toolbox, building a foundation of emotional intelligence, resilience, and multidisciplinary skills.

Pearl Slippers: The Power Was Always Within Me

Just as Dorothy discovered the power of her slippers, I came to understand that I already had the abilities I needed to navigate my path. Emotional intelligence allowed me to find meaning in every role, and resilience kept me moving forward despite the detours. I realized that my purpose wasn't tied to a specific title like "Dr. Shirita the Psychologist." Instead, it was about helping people—whether through coaching, mentoring, or creating opportunities for growth.

Discovering My True Passion and Purpose

By 25, I paused to reflect on my seven-year journey. Emotional intelligence helped me connect the dots between my experiences, while resilience helped me embrace the twists and turns. I realized that my happiest moments weren't tied to a specific career path but to meaningful action. Whether mentoring students, guiding employees, or building teams, I found fulfillment in empowering others to succeed.

Looking back, the connections created by these roles became clear:

- Therapy and psychology data collection deepened my understanding of human behavior, data analytics, and evidence-based practices.
- Coaching, leadership training, and development taught me to nurture potential and inspire growth.
- Compliance and safety showed me the value of creating structured, secure environments.

- Recruiting and marketing honed my ability to connect with people and communicate their value.

Each role wasn't a deviation from my path—it was my path. These experiences gave me a competitive advantage, an interdisciplinary lens, and the emotional intelligence to navigate life's complexities.

The Bigger Picture: The Yellow Brick Road as Purpose

Every tornado, detour, and challenge brought me closer to discovering my true purpose. The lessons reminded me that purpose isn't a fixed destination but an evolving experience. Emotional intelligence and resilience were my pearl slippers, guiding me back to my purpose at every step of the way.

My yellow brick road wasn't about becoming Dr. Shirita the Psychologist—it was about becoming the best version of myself, equipped to help others along their own journeys. And while my journey took seven years, I recognize that finding purpose can happen at any stage of life. Whether you're 18, 38, or 68, your yellow brick road is uniquely yours—and it will lead you to a life of meaning, growth, and fulfillment.

The journey down the yellow brick road isn't just about the places you visit or the milestones you achieve—it's about uncovering what truly matters and why. As my own story shows, purpose and meaning are the forces that transform even the most unexpected detours into opportunities for growth and discovery. But what exactly are purpose and meaning? Why do they matter so much in shaping the way we live and thrive? To truly understand their power, let's explore how these two essential elements give life its direction, depth, and significance.

What Are Meaning and Purpose?

Life without purpose and meaning is like driving without a GPS—sure, you're moving, but where are you even going? Without them, the days can feel like an endless loop of meaningless tasks, and even the smallest obstacles can leave you stuck in neutral. Purpose gives you direction. *What am I here to do?* Meaning helps you understand why the journey matters in the first place. *Why does this matter to me?* Together, they're the secret ingredients that turn a bland existence into a life full of vibrancy, resilience, and a sense of fulfillment (Goleman, 1995; Pink, 2009).

Finding Your "Why"

Daniel Goleman, the emotional intelligence expert (see also chapters 1, 4, and 7), explains that purpose is the fuel that powers your life's engine. It's what gets you out of bed on Monday mornings (well, most of them) and gives your actions a sense of alignment with your values. Without it, even the most productive day can feel hollow. Meaning, on the other hand, connects your goals to your emotional core, adding richness and depth to everything you do. Together, they don't just help you live—they help you thrive (Goleman, 1995).

Your Inner Compass

The Mason Resilience Model (see also chapters 2, 4, and 5) frames meaning and purpose as key elements of bouncing back from life's inevitable chaos. Meaning helps you find clarity in life's messiest moments (like when your carefully crafted five-year plan takes a nosedive), while purpose gives you the drive to dust yourself off and keep moving. It's like having an emotional compass that keeps you grounded, even when the tornadoes of life try to blow you off course.

The Productivity Booster

Dan Pink, the author of *Drive*, makes the case that purpose isn't just a feel-good concept—it's a productivity powerhouse. When you have purpose, even the most mundane tasks (hello, replying to emails) become part of a bigger picture. Purpose keeps you focused, motivated, and committed to long-term goals, even when the daily grind feels like a slog. In Pink's world, purpose isn't a luxury—it's essential for living a life of meaning and impact (Pink, 2009).

Why Purpose and Meaning Matter

When meaning and purpose team up, they turn life's challenges into opportunities and give you a reason to keep going, even when the road ahead feels uncertain. Meaning is the lens that helps you find clarity in the chaos, while purpose keeps you moving forward with determination. Together, they transform life from merely existing into truly living (Goleman, 1995; GMU Resilience Model, 2023).

So whether you're on a mission to change the world or just trying to find joy in the small things, meaning and purpose are the ultimate companions. They make the detours worthwhile, turn struggles into stories of resilience, and ensure that even the most ordinary days are filled with extraordinary potential.

Like a locked door, purpose and meaning hold the promise of fulfillment, but it takes effort and persistence to craft the key that fits. They give life direction, but unlocking them requires navigating life's twists and turns.

Let's explore how this journey reveals growth, resilience, and self-discovery.

Unlocking the Door to Purpose

On one side of the locked door to purpose and fulfillment, there's uncertainty, self-doubt, and the nagging question, *What am I meant to do*? On the other side is clarity, alignment, and the deeply satisfying moment when everything falls into place. It is like there is a partition separating you from a life of fulfillment. But here's the twist: The key to that door isn't handed to you. You have to find it, shape it, and sometimes, even forge it yourself.

Imagine starting your journey with a clear vision—perhaps you wanted to be a teacher, a writer, or an entrepreneur. It seemed

straightforward at first, but life has a way of tossing in unexpected detours. You might find yourself exploring paths you never anticipated, like moving from a creative role to corporate management or shifting from a career in sales to education. Each step along the way, though it may feel like a diversion, is actually adding notches to the key you're crafting.

The Search for the Right Fit

If you've ever struggled with a stubborn lock and the wrong key, you understand how the journey to purpose can feel. You try, you adjust, and you wonder if you'll ever find the right fit. Perhaps you took a job you weren't sure about, started a side hustle, or went back to school. Each role, each experience—no matter how seemingly disconnected—teaches you something new.

For example, working in customer service might teach you patience and communication. A stint in marketing could hone your ability to connect with others. A brief foray into project management might help you learn structure and organization. These aren't wasted efforts; they're shaping your key, sharpening it until it can finally unlock the door. It's not about one single role or experience—it's the accumulation of all of them.

What's on the Other Side?

When you finally find the right key, the door opens to a life where your passions, skills, and values align. On the other side, you may realize that it's not about a specific title or job but about how you make an impact. Whether it's mentoring others, creating something meaningful, or contributing to your community, purpose reveals itself in the actions that resonate deeply with you.

That doesn't mean the journey stops there. Unlocking one door often leads to another, and new challenges will arise. But that first unlocked door proves that persistence pays off. It shows you that the journey—the missteps, the lessons, and the moments of doubt—is just as valuable as the destination.

Crafting Your Key

If you're still searching for your key, take heart—it's a process that requires patience and resilience. Finding your purpose isn't about waiting for a perfect opportunity to fall into your lap. It's about embracing the process of trial and error. Each job you take, each project you try, even each failure, is shaping the key that will one day fit the lock.

So, keep exploring, keep learning, and keep moving forward. The key to your door is already in the making, and when it clicks, the life waiting on the other side will be worth every twist, turn, and unexpected detour it took to get there.

Unlocking the door to purpose isn't the end of the journey—it's the beginning of a life enriched by meaning, direction, and growth. As you craft your key through exploration and persistence, each moment offers an opportunity for reflection and intentional action.

Now, let's turn insight into practice with an activity designed to help you dive deeper into your personal sense of purpose and meaning.

Reflection

Purpose and Meaning in Life

Discovering purpose and meaning in life isn't a straightforward journey—it's more like assembling a puzzle with pieces you gather through experiences, challenges, and self-discovery. As you navigate your own path, reflection becomes a powerful tool for understanding where you've been, where you are, and where you're headed. Get your notebook, sit in a quiet place, and create the mental space for personal self-reflection. These questions are designed to help you think deeply, evaluate your current trajectory, and take intentional action toward uncovering your purpose and living a meaningful life.

Think (Understanding & Awareness)

Consider these questions to explore your current understanding:

1. What does the concept of purpose mean to you personally, and how do you define it in your own life?
2. Reflect on a moment when life felt especially meaningful. What contributed to that feeling?
3. How do you currently describe the difference between living with purpose and simply going through the motions?
4. What are three values you hold most dear, and how do they influence your decisions and actions?
5. What life experiences have shaped your understanding of meaning and purpose the most?

Evaluate (Analyzing & Reflecting)

Take time to analyze and reflect on your emotional habits and patterns:

1. Think about a time when you felt "stuck" or unsure about your path. How did you navigate through it, and what did you learn?
2. Are there recurring themes or patterns in the things that make you feel fulfilled? What might those patterns reveal about your purpose?
3. How does the work you currently do—or the life you currently lead—align with your values and passions?
4. When you consider past challenges, how have they contributed to your personal growth or understanding of your purpose?

5. Are there areas in your life where your actions and values feel misaligned? If so, how might you bring them closer together?

Act (Implementation & Practice)

Turn your reflections into action with these practical steps:

1. What small step can you take this week to align your daily actions with your values?
2. Identify one skill or strength you've gained from a past experience. How might you use it to contribute to a meaningful cause or goal?
3. How can you intentionally create moments of reflection in your routine to check in on your journey toward purpose?
4. What's one challenge you're facing now, and how can you reframe it as an opportunity to grow or gain clarity?
5. Write down one action you will take to move closer to uncovering or living out your purpose, no matter how small it may seem.

These questions are not about finding immediate answers—they're about starting a conversation with yourself, uncovering insights, and embracing the journey of discovery. Purpose and meaning evolve over time, and the more you reflect and act, the clearer your path will become. Remember, every small step you take brings you closer to unlocking the door to a life of fulfillment and impact.

Reflection is a powerful tool for uncovering purpose and aligning your actions with your values. By examining your journey, identifying patterns, and considering where you're headed, you can gain clarity about what truly matters. But, understanding is just the first step.

Now, let's take it a step further with a creative and forward-looking activity: imagining your retirement. This exercise will help you envision the legacy you want to leave behind and inspire actionable steps to start building it today.

Activity

Your Retirement Celebration—Crafting Your Legacy

This activity invites you to imagine your ideal retirement celebration, filled with friends, family, and colleagues reflecting on the incredible journey of your life and career. It's a chance to dream about the impact you want to have and the values you'll be remembered for—and to recognize how your actions today align with your vision for tomorrow. Use the worksheet below to record your thoughts.

Let's celebrate what a life well-lived looks like!

Steps to Craft Your Retirement Celebration

1. Set the Scene

Picture your retirement party—a joyous occasion where people gather to honor your achievements and legacy. Who is at your celebration, and what does the atmosphere feel like?

Examples: Family, friends, coworkers, mentees, community members, music, laughter.

____

____

____

2. Define Your Impact

Imagine what people will say when they talk about the mark you've left on their lives. What difference did you make? What do you hope people celebrate about your contributions and impact?

Examples: Leading a team to success, mentoring future leaders, making a difference in your community, inspiring others.

____

____

____

3. Identify Key Values

Consider the values that guided your journey—these are the principles that people will recognize as part of your legacy. What values do you want people to highlight when they reflect on your career and life?

Examples: Integrity, creativity, kindness, resilience, humor, passion.

____

____

____

4. Celebrate Accomplishments

Reflect on the achievements you want celebrated at your retirement. These could be personal, professional, or even playful! What milestones will people toast to at your retirement celebration?

Examples: A successful career, personal growth, mentoring others, building a loving family, traveling the world, creating something meaningful.

____

____

____

5. Highlight Relationships

Relationships are often the most cherished parts of our lives. How do you want people to describe the connections they had with you? How do you hope people will remember the way you made them feel?

Examples: Encouraged, supported, inspired, cared for, appreciated.

____

____

____

Write Your Retirement Speech

Imagine giving a heartfelt speech at your celebration. Summarize the legacy you've created, the values you've upheld, and the gratitude you feel.

____

____

____

Template for Your Retirement Speech

"Thank you all for being here to celebrate this milestone with me. As I look back on my journey, I'm filled with gratitude for the experiences I've had, the lessons I've learned, and the amazing people I've met along the way.

I'm proud to have lived by [key values] and to have contributed by [impact or accomplishments]. Whether it was through [specific examples of contributions], my goal has always been to [legacy or purpose].

The relationships I've built have been the most meaningful part of my journey. To me, life is about [reflection on relationships or connection], and I'm so thankful for everyone who has been part of this adventure.

As I move into this new chapter, I carry with me the lessons, laughter, and love that have shaped my life. Here's to continuing the journey with purpose, joy, and the incredible support of all of you. Thank you for being part of my story."

Your Speech:

Reflection Questions

1. How does your current life align with the vision of your ideal retirement celebration?

____

____

____

2. What's one action you can take today to work toward the legacy you want to create?

____

____

____

3. How can you celebrate small wins and meaningful moments on your journey to this vision?

____

____

____

This exercise isn't about achieving perfection—it's about setting an inspiring vision for your future and aligning your actions with your values. Your retirement celebration can serve as a joyful reminder to live each day with purpose and meaning.

Ending for Chapter 8: Purpose and Meaning in Life

Purpose and meaning transform our lives from a series of tasks and challenges into a vibrant journey filled with passion, resilience, and fulfillment. They guide us through the twists and turns, give us strength in moments of doubt, and help us embrace every detour as part of a larger story.

As we reflect on the journey to discovering our "why," we are reminded that purpose is not a final destination; it's an ever-evolving experience shaped by who we are and how we connect with the world. Whether through small daily actions or grand lifetime achievements, purpose helps us live intentionally, while meaning gives our actions depth and significance.

The process of crafting a purposeful life requires emotional intelligence and resilience—the courage to adapt, the wisdom to reflect, and the heart to remain true to our values. These are the qualities that will guide us in the next chapter, where we'll explore how leadership intertwines with emotional intelligence and resilience. Together, these elements empower us to inspire, uplift, and lead not just ourselves, but those around us, toward meaningful growth and success.

As we close out this chapter, proceed to the next chapter or navigate to the chapter that feels most meaningful for you. Chapter 9 dives into the power of leadership with emotional intelligence and resilience. We will explore how these skills help us lead with purpose, navigate challenges, and create a lasting impact.

Chapter 9

Leadership 101—A Masterclass from Unlikely Mentors

- UNCONVENTIONAL MENTORS
- PROFILE 1: THE MICROMANAGER WITH SELECTIVE AMNESIA
- PROFILE 2: THE PERFECTIONIST TYRANT
- PROFILE 3: THE OVERCOMMITTER
- PROFILE 4: THE FEARFUL GATEKEEPER
- PROFILE 5: THE WHAT-HAVE-YOU-DONE-FOR-ME-LATELY? LEADER
- REFLECTION: MASTERCLASS FROM UNLIKELY MENTORS
- ACTIVITY: LEADERSHIP PERSONA

9

Leadership 101—A Masterclass From Unlikely Mentors

"It is the leaders who decide what kind of environment they want to build."
— Simon Sinek

Have you ever stopped to consider the environment you create for those around you? What kind of culture are your actions and decisions shaping—one of trust and growth, or one of fear and control? Every interaction, choice, and reaction sends a message about your values and priorities as a leader. Whether intentional or not, the environment you foster has a direct impact on the well-being, motivation, and performance of the people you lead.

Leadership comes in many forms, and a leader isn't confined to a specific title or position. A leader can be anyone who influences, guides, or inspires others in meaningful ways. Examples of leaders include parents nurturing their children, teachers shaping young minds, managers guiding their teams, clergy providing spiritual support, coaches motivating their players, mentors offering guidance, community organizers driving change, and even friends who lend support and encouragement in times of need.

Leadership is not just about tasks and directives; it's about crafting the culture and environment that defines how people function and thrive. A leader's decisions—both big and small—shape the atmosphere of collaboration, trust, and growth within their sphere of influence. When leaders prioritize empathy, care, and empowerment, they create an environment where people feel valued and motivated. Conversely, a lack of intentionality in leadership can lead to dysfunction, distrust, and missed potential.

This idea came into sharp focus during my encounters with what I now call "unconventional mentors." These were leaders who, through their missteps, taught me some of the most enduring lessons about leadership. Their environments were often marked by control, perfectionism, and a lack of trust, which made it clear how vital care and emotional intelligence are in fostering connection and collaboration.

A leader's environment is their legacy. The culture they build not only affects immediate outcomes but also the long-term development of the people they lead. My experiences with these unconventional mentors shaped my commitment to creating environments rooted in emotional intelligence and resilience—spaces where people feel supported, valued, and inspired to grow.

The Turning Points: The "Unconventional Mentors"

Leadership lessons are often forged in the fire of difficult experiences, and for me, those lessons came from working under a variety of challenging bosses—each with their own unique style of dysfunction. These leaders weren't bad people; they were just unequipped with the tools of emotional intelligence and resilience that make a leader truly effective. What they lacked in empathy, adaptability, and trust, they made up for in micromanagement, perfectionism, and misplaced priorities. While working for them wasn't always easy, the lessons they inadvertently taught me became the foundation of my own leadership journey.

Through these experiences, I learned what leadership should not look like: hovering over every task like a helicopter parent, demanding unattainable perfection without offering support, or avoiding conflict to the detriment of the team. These "unconventional mentors" unknowingly provided me with a roadmap—by showing me the wrong turns to avoid. This chapter captures those turning points, diving into the profiles of the leaders who left a lasting impression on me, for better or worse.

What I gained from these experiences wasn't just frustration—it was insight. Each encounter highlighted the power of emotional intelligence in leadership: the ability to connect with others, adapt to challenges, and foster trust. And each story reinforced the importance of resilience, both for surviving under challenging leaders and for growing into a better one myself.

The manager personas described in the next section are composites created from a combination of traits and experiences drawn from various unconventional mentors. They are not intended to represent specific individuals but rather to illustrate key leadership dynamics and lessons.

Let's take a closer look at the behavior traits that have shaped my understanding of what it means to truly lead.

Profile 1: The Micromanager With Selective Amnesia (aka Ms. and Mr. Control-It-All)

Ms. and Mr. Control-It-All had an extraordinary gift for turning every project into a collaborative nightmare. They hovered over every task like a helicopter stuck on autopilot, questioning every decision, demanding multiple unnecessary revisions, and sprinkling in unsolicited advice like it was fairy dust. Unfortunately, this "advice" often led to chaos, and when things went sideways, their selective amnesia kicked in. Suddenly, the bad ideas weren't theirs, and the consequences became my problem.

They talked to me like I was a wayward toddler, not a professional with valuable insights. They would issue a steady stream of instructions punctuated by their go-to mantras: "Let me show you the right way", "I know what works", "You need to be careful." I vividly remember one presentation they made me redo three times. We ended up using my original version, but do you think they acknowledged my effort or success? Nope. They acted as if the final product magically appeared out of thin air, with them leading the charge.

How Emotional Intelligence Could Have Helped:

Ms. and Mr. Control-It-All could have harnessed emotional intelligence by practicing trust, humility, and self-awareness. Instead of micromanaging, they could have empowered their team by delegating tasks with clear expectations and recognizing individual contributions. When mistakes happened (even their own), owning them and fostering an environment of learning would have built trust. Leaders with emotional intelligence understand the value of collaboration and the morale boost that comes with sharing credit and giving constructive feedback without condescension.

Learned Lessons:

If you find yourself becoming a Ms. and Mr. Control-It-All, remember that great leadership is built on trust, respect, and the ability to let go. Emotional intelligence means empowering your team, recognizing their strengths, and creating a space where creativity and confidence can thrive. Resilience, on the other hand, means finding ways to keep motivation alive—and realizing that micromanagement says more about a leader's insecurities than the team's capabilities.

Profile 2: The Perfectionist Tyrant (aka Ms. and Mr. No Work-Life Balance)

Ms. and Mr. No Work-Life Balance demanded excellence without compromise, a combination that created a pressure-cooker environment where every task felt like a test of survival. Their expectations were sky-high, but their support? Practically nonexistent. They'd assign massive projects with unrealistic deadlines and then vanish, leaving us to figure out how to make it happen. Recognition for effort or progress was unheard of—unless, of course, you counted their curt "Well, you should have done that anyway" or "It is about time" as praise.

Their motto? "I don't care if it takes you 60 hours to get this done—we're only paying you for 40. Work-life balance? Never heard of it." They operated with an iron fist and a severe lack of empathy, creating an environment where burnout wasn't a possibility—it was a guarantee. The kicker? They once criticized a colleague for missing a deadline on a project delayed because of their own last-minute demands. Perfection wasn't just the goal; it was the only acceptable option, and falling short wasn't met with understanding but with finger-pointing and passive-aggressive comments.

How Emotional Intelligence Could Have Helped:

Ms. and Mr. No Work-Life Balance could have transformed their leadership style with a dose of empathy and adaptability. By setting realistic expectations and acknowledging the team's efforts along the way, they could have fostered a more supportive environment. Celebrating progress—even when the final result wasn't perfect—would have boosted morale and built trust. Leaders with emotional intelligence recognize that perfection is unattainable and that focusing on growth and collaboration yields better outcomes than fear-driven leadership.

Learned Lessons:

In moments when you feel like a Ms. and Mr. No Work-Life Balance, remind yourself to celebrate small wins and recognize effort, not just outcomes. Leadership isn't about unattainable standards; it's about setting your team up for success and appreciating their contributions. Resilience came into play as I learned to adapt to unreasonable demands and find ways to maintain my sanity while meeting expectations. And perhaps most importantly, I realized that valuing work-life balance is crucial—for both the team's productivity and their well-being.

Profile 3: The Yes, Overcommitter (aka Ms. and Mr. People-Pleaser)

Ms. and Mr. People-Pleaser had a heart that belonged in a Hallmark movie, but their decision-making skills were better suited to a game show where every answer is "yes." When our team of ten was abruptly slashed down to four, they responded to the crisis by agreeing to every project, initiative, and request that came their way. "Teamwork makes the dream work" and "We've got this!" they'd say, exuding an optimism that might have been charming—if it wasn't so wildly unrealistic. Spoiler alert: We absolutely did not "have this."

Under their leadership, our days turned into a relentless game of "what fire do we put out first?" They avoided conflict with upper management like it was a high-stakes game of dodgeball, refusing to push back on impossible demands or advocate for more resources. Deadlines flew by unmet, morale nosedived, and "team effort" became a cruel punchline when the "team" was just me and three colleagues desperately trying to do the work of ten.

How Emotional Intelligence Could Have Helped:

If Ms. and Mr. People-Pleaser had used emotional intelligence, they would have realized that leadership is about prioritization and protecting your team—not bending to every demand to avoid conflict. Self-awareness could have helped them recognize their people-pleasing tendencies, while empathy and social awareness would have shown them the toll their decisions were taking on the team. With emotional intelligence, they could have communicated boundaries effectively, advocated for the team's needs, and modeled resilience by setting realistic expectations. A leader who says "no" or "not right now" when possible builds trust, prevents burnout, and ensures long-term success.

Learned Lessons:

Should you realize you are acting like a Ms. and Mr. People-Pleaser, remember that leadership isn't about avoiding hard conversations or making everyone happy—it's about making decisions that prioritize the well-being of your team and the success of the organization. Emotional intelligence in leadership means understanding capacity, saying "no", "not right now", and "here are the downstream effects" with grace, and having the courage to advocate for what's realistic. Resilience, for me, came from finding humor in the chaos, staying focused on what I could control, and learning that boundaries are not just helpful—they're essential. True leaders know that sometimes the best way to say "yes" to your team is by questioning the impossible.

Profile 4: The Fearful Gatekeeper (aka Ms. and Mr. Status Quo)

Ms. and Mr. Status Quo were the leaders who feared change more than anything else. They clung to outdated methods and made decisions based on comfort, not progress. Their catch phrase might as well have been, "We've always done it this way." When faced with innovative ideas or promising opportunities, their response was usually a hesitant, "I'm not sure that's the right fit" or "it is not the right time."

One incident stands out: I proposed implementing a new cost effective technology solution to streamline a cumbersome process and enhance efficiency. My manager resisted, clinging to the outdated method, citing concerns about potential disruptions and the team's ability to adapt. I presented a strong case, secured buy-in, and moved forward with the implementation. Spoiler alert: The new system not only improved efficiency but also empowered the team to focus on higher-value tasks, ultimately exceeding expectations and delivering measurable results.

How Emotional Intelligence Could Have Helped:

Ms. and Mr. Status Quo could have used emotional intelligence to embrace adaptability and openness. By fostering curiosity instead of fear, they could have recognized the potential in new ideas and technologies. Great leaders aren't afraid to take calculated risks or step outside their comfort zones when it means growth for their team. A willingness to listen, learn, and trust others' judgment would have made them a more effective and forward-thinking leader.

Learned Lessons:

While practicing self-awareness and reflection, if you find yourself acting like a Ms. and Mr. Status Quo, remind yourself that leadership demands courage and a willingness to embrace change. For me, resilience meant standing firm in my convictions and advocating for what I believed was right, even in the face of resistance. Emotional intelligence showed me the importance of seeing potential in ideas, even when they don't fit the "traditional" mold.

Profile 5: The What-Have-You-Done-For-Me-Lately? Leader (aka Ms. and Mr. Next-Up)

Ms. and Mr. Next-Up are always laser-focused on the future, never taking the time to acknowledge or celebrate past successes. Accomplishments—no matter how significant—were quickly brushed aside with a brief "good job," followed immediately by, "So, what's next?" This relentless forward focus left me feeling like my hard work was invisible, and I was perpetually sprinting on a treadmill with no end in sight.

One particularly chaotic time stands out. I was juggling multiple high-priority projects with tight deadlines. Trying to keep all the balls in the air without dropping them, while training a new team member. Amidst this whirlwind, I was criticized for being "unresponsive" and not being a "team player" after taking a few hours to answer a Skype message—despite awaiting crucial input from two key stakeholders.

Instead of offering support or checking in, Ms. and Mr. Next-Up used the moment to lecture me about "meeting expectations" and implied I might miss out on development opportunities if I didn't step it up. Ouch. This shift caught me off guard, especially since just a week earlier, I had received a promotion based on my exceptional work ethic and results.

Looking back, I realized the tension wasn't entirely one-sided. The environment at the time was high-pressure, and Ms. and Mr. Next-Up—normally empathetic and reasonable—was likely feeling the strain, too. But as a leader, projecting stress onto your team only amplifies the problem.

How Emotional Intelligence Could Have Helped:

Ms. and Mr. Next-Up could have benefited greatly from leaning into emotional intelligence, particularly empathy and curiosity. A leader with emotional intelligence could have taken a moment to acknowledge the challenges I was facing, offering support instead of critique. What could have made a world of difference was a simple display of curiosity and understanding, like saying, "Hey, I noticed you've been slower to respond recently. Is everything okay? How can I support you?" That one question could have turned a stressful situation into a moment of collaboration.

Learned Lessons:

If the demands of your environment have you unconsciously acting like Ms. and Mr. Next-Up, remember that effective leadership isn't about constantly pushing for the next achievement—it's about balancing accountability with genuine empathy and support. There is value in recognizing and celebrating accomplishments, no matter how small, as a way to motivate and inspire teams. Emotional intelligence in leadership is about being attuned to the needs and challenges of your team, asking thoughtful questions, and fostering a culture of collaboration rather than criticism. For me, resilience meant finding ways to validate my own efforts, even when external recognition was absent, and staying focused on what I could control. This experience reinforced the idea that leaders who create environments of trust, encouragement, and acknowledgment build stronger, more engaged teams than those who operate solely on pressure and expectations. True leadership is about valuing people, not just performance.

Keeping Your Cool Under Chaos: Interacting with Challenging People

In your professional or personal life, if you find yourself interacting with a Ms. or Mr. Control-It-All, No Work-Life Balance, People-Pleaser, Status Quo, or Next-Up, applying emotional intelligence may feel like navigating a minefield—while blindfolded.

- Start with your self-awareness—acknowledge how their behavior makes you want to scream into a pillow but resist the urge to send that passive-aggressive email or block their calls.
- Lean into your empathy—embrace your secret weapon; remember, their behavior often stems from their own stress or insecurities.
- Channel self-regulation—focus on what you can control—your mindset, your humor, and your ability to survive their quirks without losing your sanity.
- Leverage your social skills—use assertive communication to set boundaries respectfully and advocate for your needs.

- Reignite your motivation— remind yourself of your goals and purpose; find ways to stay inspired despite their behavior.

By modeling emotional intelligence, you can not only navigate these challenges but maybe even inspire these people to change—maybe. And if all else fails, remember: every challenging person is teaching you what not to do when it's your turn to connect with others or lead.

Emerging as a Leader

Reflecting on these profiles of challenging leadership experiences, I can see how each shaped my understanding of what it truly means to lead. Each misstep I witnessed in others became a valuable lesson in what to avoid and what to strive for. Leadership, I learned, isn't about micromanaging, demanding perfection, avoiding conflict, resisting change, or relentlessly pushing for results without acknowledgment. It's about balance—between accountability and empathy, direction and trust, and expectations and support.

One pivotal moment where these lessons crystallized for me was during a particularly demanding project. Our team faced tight deadlines, competing priorities, and a sense of burnout that hung in the air like a fog. It would have been easy to fall into the traps I'd seen in my past leaders—doubling down on criticism, piling on the pressure, or brushing off the team's concerns. Instead, I consciously chose a different path.

I started by acknowledging the hard work everyone was putting in and openly recognizing small wins along the way. I took the time to listen to my team's frustrations and brainstorm solutions collaboratively, rather than dictating what should be done. When mistakes happened, I reframed them as learning opportunities and encouraged resilience rather than assigning blame. Most importantly,

I made space for humor and humanity during our most stressful moments—reminding everyone (myself included) that we were more than our productivity.

What made the difference? Emotional intelligence and resilience. By tuning into my team's needs and maintaining a steady focus on what mattered most, I created an environment of trust and camaraderie, even under pressure. That project wasn't just a success—it became a turning point in my own leadership journey. It proved to me that leadership is less about authority and more about influence, connection, and the ability to inspire others to thrive.

These lessons continue to guide me, not just as a leader but as a person. Leadership is a journey, not a title, and every challenge presents an opportunity to grow. As I've come to understand, it's not the difficult experiences themselves that define us—it's how we rise from them, armed with new insights and the courage to lead with integrity.

Leadership is a constant balancing act—managing not just tasks and outcomes, but the emotions, strengths, and challenges of the people who make up your team. It's about taking the lessons learned from past challenges and applying them in a way that fosters trust, collaboration, and growth. But how do you bring all these moving parts together seamlessly? The answer lies in adopting the perspective of a symphony conductor, harmonizing emotional intelligence and resilience to create something greater than the sum of its parts.

Leadership: The Symphony Conductor of Emotional Intelligence and Resilience

Leadership, much like conducting a symphony, involves orchestrating chaos into something harmonious—except your "musicians" are

people with varying moods, opinions, and, occasionally, a penchant for playing their own tune. Picture yourself as the conductor, baton in hand, trying to bring together a team that sometimes feels more like a kazoo concert than a world-class orchestra. It's a wild ride, but with emotional intelligence and resilience, you can turn the cacophony into a masterpiece.

Emotional Intelligence: The Maestro's Magic Wand

A conductor doesn't bark orders at the violins or scold the percussionists for being too enthusiastic with their cymbals (okay, maybe once). Instead, they understand that each instrument—and each musician—has its own quirks. Similarly, a leader with emotional intelligence listens carefully, like a maestro tuning in to the clarinet's subtle flat note or the trumpet's overzealous solo.

Have a team member who always hits the wrong "note" in meetings? Emotional intelligence helps you guide them with empathy instead of frustration. It's about knowing when to encourage a shy "flutist" (team member) to step into the spotlight and when to gently suggest that your "drummer" (the overly talkative one) might benefit from a brief pause. And when your team inevitably hits a sour note—like missing a deadline or sending an email reply-all—emotional intelligence helps you strike the right chord: understanding and constructive feedback, not public shaming.

Resilience: The Conductor's Poker Face

Let's be honest, not every symphony (or team project) goes off without a hitch. Sometimes, the cellos forget their part, the timpani comes in early, and the trumpets just won't stop improvising. A resilient conductor doesn't throw their baton in frustration; they roll with it, signaling confidently for the orchestra to keep going like it was all part of the plan.

In leadership, resilience is your ability to handle the equivalent of your bassoon player calling in sick mid-performance. Maybe the printer breaks five minutes before a client presentation, or your team's "star violinist" (read: key contributor) takes an unexpected vacation during crunch time. Resilience is laughing instead of crying, pivoting instead of panicking, and showing your team that even when the cymbals crash a little too hard, the show will go on.

Conducting Harmony (Or Something Close to It)

When emotional intelligence and resilience join forces, you create harmony—or at least something that resembles it if you squint hard enough. It's not about achieving perfection. The trombone will inevitably play a wrong note, and someone in the woodwinds will sneeze at the worst possible moment. But as a leader, you inspire your team to keep playing, recover with grace, and remember that even the hiccups add charm to the performance.

As the conductor of your own leadership symphony, the beauty lies not in achieving flawless execution but in how you guide your team through the inevitable missteps and surprises. Emotional intelligence and resilience are your most powerful tools, helping you navigate the discord with grace and turn challenges into opportunities for growth. Now, it's your turn to reflect on the lessons you've learned and the leadership style you aspire to embody. The following activity will help you dive deeper into your experiences, uncover insights, and take actionable steps to fine-tune your leadership approach, ensuring your team plays in harmony—even if the occasional kazoo moment sneaks in.

Reflection

Masterclass From Unlikely Mentors

Leadership is a journey of growth, shaped not just by our successes but also by the challenges we face and the lessons we learn from others—especially those who unintentionally show us what not to do. Reflecting on these experiences can illuminate our own leadership styles and uncover areas for growth. Pick up your journal, retreat to a calm environment, and invite curiosity into your thoughts. The following questions are designed to help you think deeply about your own experiences, evaluate your approach to leadership, and take actionable steps to lead with emotional intelligence and resilience. Use this as an opportunity to pause, reflect, and align your leadership practices with your values and aspirations.

Think (Understanding & Awareness)

Consider these questions to explore your current understanding:

1. How would you describe your current leadership style?
2. Can you recall a time when a leader made you feel valued and supported? What did they do?
3. Reflect on a challenging leadership experience you've had. What emotions did it bring up, and how did you handle them?
4. What does emotional intelligence mean to you, and how do you see it playing a role in leadership?
5. Think about a time when you felt micromanaged or unsupported. How did it impact your performance and morale?

Evaluate (Analyzing & Reflecting)

Take time to analyze and reflect on your emotional habits and patterns:

1. When observing leaders in your past, what qualities stood out as the most effective or inspiring?
2. Identify a moment when you witnessed or experienced poor leadership. What could have been done differently to improve the situation?
3. Are there patterns or behaviors in your leadership that reflect those you've admired or found frustrating in others?
4. How do you currently balance accountability with empathy in your leadership approach?

5. Think about a time when a mistake was made on your team. How was it handled, and what did it teach you about fostering resilience?

Act (Implementation & Practice)

Turn your reflections into action with these practical steps:

1. What's one action you can take this week to build trust with your team?

2. Identify a situation where you can practice emotional intelligence—whether by listening actively, showing empathy, or giving constructive feedback.

3. How can you celebrate small wins with your team to boost morale and encourage progress?

4. Commit to one area of growth as a leader (e.g., delegation, active listening, setting boundaries). What first step can you take toward improvement?

5. Reflecting on the lessons you've learned from past leaders, how can you apply them to create a more supportive and effective team environment?

As you reflect on your experiences with leadership—both the inspiring moments and the challenges—you begin to uncover the values, strengths, and areas of growth that shape your unique leadership style. The lessons learned from observing others and navigating your own leadership journey provide a foundation for self-awareness. Now, it's time to take that reflection a step further by exploring your leadership persona. This activity will help you connect with your core motivations, identify potential pitfalls, and develop strategies to lead with emotional intelligence and resilience. Through this deeper self-discovery, you'll gain the clarity needed to lead with intention and authenticity, creating a positive and lasting impact on those you serve.

Activity

Your Leadership Persona, Leaning Into Emotional Intelligence and Resilience

Great leadership starts with self-awareness. Understanding who you are as a leader—your motivations, strengths, fears, and opportunities—forms the foundation for growth and adaptability. This activity is designed to help you create a personalized leadership persona, offering insights into your natural style while identifying potential pitfalls. By reflecting on these aspects, you'll develop strategies to avoid unproductive behaviors and leverage emotional intelligence and resilience to stay balanced and effective. Leadership isn't about being perfect—it's about growing with intention, learning from challenges, and leading with authenticity. Use the worksheet below to guide your self-discovery journey, helping you develop a mindful and impactful approach to leadership.

Step 1: Define Your Leadership Persona

Answer the following questions to map out your leadership persona. Write your responses in the corresponding sections.

1. What's your leadership style?

Think about how you typically approach leading others. Are you task-focused, relationship-driven, or big-picture-oriented?

___

___

___

2. What motivates you as a leader? What are your core needs as a leader?

Identify the key drivers behind your leadership. This could be recognition, achieving results, collaboration, or making an impact.

___

___

___

3. What are your biggest fears as a leader?

Reflect on the concerns that might hold you back. Are you afraid of failure, rejection, losing control, or appearing inadequate?

___

___

___

4. What are your greatest leadership opportunities?

Highlight areas where you have potential for growth. Do you struggle with handling conflict or delegating important tasks?

Step 2: Recognize Potential Traps

Using your answers from Step 1, consider how each aspect of your leadership persona might lead to unproductive behaviors or potential pitfalls. Write down your thoughts in the corresponding sections.

1. Too much of your leadership style:

How could leaning too far into your style become a weakness? For example, being overly task-oriented might lead to neglecting relationships.

2. Not feeling motivated or not getting your needs met:

How might unmet needs or low motivation impact your effectiveness? For example, needing recognition might cause frustration when it's lacking.

3. Avoiding your fears:

How might avoiding your fears lead to unproductive behaviors? For example, fear of failure might lead to micromanaging or indecision.

4. What happens when you avoid addressing opportunities?

How might neglecting growth opportunities hold you back as a leader?

Step 3: Emotional Intelligence and Resilience in Action

For each potential trap identified in Step 2, outline specific ways you can use emotional intelligence and resilience to stay balanced. Write your responses below:

Too much of your leadership style:

How will you practice self-awareness to recognize when your style is becoming unproductive?

How can you use adaptibility to adjust your approach?

Not feeling motivated or getting your needs met:

How can you use self-regulation to manage frustration and maintain focus?

How can you use intrinsic motivations to stay driven?

EMOTIONAL INTELLIGENCE AND RESILIENCE IN ACTION

Avoiding your fears:

How will you use self-confidence to face fears and take risks?

How can you build resilience to recover from setbacks?

Addressing leadership opportunities:

How can you use social awareness to identify opportunities for growth?

How will you use relationship management to build collaboration and trust?

Step 4: Final Reflection

Answer the following reflection questions based on your completed leadership persona:

1. What did you learn about yourself as a leader through this exercise?

2. How can you leverage emotional intelligence to become a more balanced and effective leader?

3. What specific strategies will you use to maintain resilience in challenging leadership moments?

4. What is one leadership behavior or mindset you want to adopt moving forward?

Ending for Chapter 9: Leadership 101—A Masterclass From Unlikely Mentors

Leadership is not a destination—it's an evolving journey, shaped by the lessons we learn, the challenges we face, and the connections we build with those we lead. The unconventional mentors and their shortcomings may have shown us what leadership shouldn't look like, but they also provided invaluable insights into what it truly means to lead with emotional intelligence and resilience.

By reflecting on these experiences and cultivating self-awareness, we gain the clarity and tools to refine our own leadership styles. As we step into the role of leaders, it's not about achieving perfection but embracing growth, balancing accountability with empathy, and inspiring those around us to thrive.

In the next chapter, we'll explore how to build, nurture, and empower teams with the same principles of emotional intelligence and resilience. Together, let's learn how to create a culture of collaboration, trust, and shared success—because great leadership doesn't happen in isolation; it thrives in the collective.

Or, follow your instincts and dive into the chapter that feels most aligned with your current situation.

Chapter 10

Cultivating a Resilient Team

- TRANSFORMING TENSIONS INTO TEAM
- RESILIENCE: A JOURNEY OF GROWTH
- REFLECTION: BUILDING RESILIENT TEAMS
- TEAM ACTIVITY: ALL ABOUT ME

10

Cultivating a Resilient Team

"Talent wins games, but teamwork and intelligence win championships."
—Michael Jordan

Have you ever been part of a team where everything just clicked—where trust, collaboration, and shared purpose seemed to flow effortlessly? Or, have you experienced the frustration of being on a team where tension and miscommunication held everyone back? Teams can come in all shapes and forms—couples in a relationship, co-parents navigating family dynamics, close-knit families, church groups, sports teams, dance ensembles, workplace teams, sororities, fraternities, volunteer organizations, and more. At its core, a team is a group of individuals working together toward a common goal. But not all teams function the same way.

Michael Jordan's iconic quote is a reminder that individual brilliance can take you far, but it's the collective effort of a team that leads to sustained success. When it comes to building resilient teams, this quote holds profound relevance. Teams are not simply collections of skilled individuals; they are dynamic systems where collaboration, trust, and communication turn raw talent into championship results. In basketball, as in life, every player brings unique strengths and roles to the game. However, it's the synergy of those efforts, guided by strategy and emotional intelligence, that transforms potential into greatness. And let's be honest—there's no "I" in team, but there is one in "win," so balance matters.

Talent can help you win the day, but emotional intelligence and teamwork are what carry a group through setbacks, challenges, and adversity. A resilient team thrives not because every individual is flawless but because they learn how to support one another, leverage strengths, and bounce back stronger from obstacles. Emotional intelligence is the glue that binds such teams together—it fosters empathy, clear communication, and the ability to navigate conflict constructively. Because, let's face it, a team without emotional intelligence is just a group chat waiting to go off the rails.

As leaders, creating a resilient team means understanding that it's not enough to have skilled individuals. You must cultivate an environment where team members feel safe to contribute, fail, and grow. It means building connections based on trust, and inspiring collaboration that goes beyond personal gain. Just as championships are not won in a single game, resilient teams are not built overnight—they are the result of continuous effort, reflection, and adaptation. Jordan's words challenge us to think beyond individual accomplishments and focus on the bigger picture. Whether in the workplace, a marriage, a community, or a sports team, the real "championships" are achieved when we learn to work together with emotional intelligence and resilience as our foundation. And remember, no one wants to be the most valuable player of a losing team.

Building a resilient team isn't just about setting goals—it's about addressing the underlying dynamics that can either propel a team forward or hold it back. When tensions go unspoken and trust wavers, even the most talented teams struggle to reach their full potential. This is where emotional intelligence and resilience become transformative forces. My work with several such teams exemplifies how these principles can turn simmering conflict into meaningful connection and collaboration, laying the foundation for lasting growth. The following is a combination of organizational development and coaching support for several teams. For illustrative purposes, these experiences are referred to as one group's experience.

Transforming Tensions Into Team Resilience: A Journey of Growth

As a coach and facilitator for a team retreat, I worked with a group achieving their goals on paper but struggling with trust, authenticity, and collaboration. As I designed the retreat, I followed the best practice of organizational development: engaging with the client at each stage to discuss why certain actions should occur in respect to the broader strategic framework (Nash & Bricka, 2023). This approach ensured that every activity and intervention aligned with the team's long-term goals, fostering a sense of ownership and reinforcing the retreat's focus on building trust and resilience.

Through one-on-one meetings with each team member, I uncovered underlying tensions and miscommunications that hindered their cohesion. These insights shaped a retreat focused on emotional intelligence, trust-building, and improved communication.

To guide this team, I leaned on Tuckman's stages of team development, a framework to understand the stages a team goes through on its journey to becoming high performing:

- Forming or testing, the initial stage where group members test what behaviors are accepted by the group
- Storming or conflicting, a period of role and personality clashes
- Norming or cohering, a period of harmony and role acceptance
- Performing or functioning, a period of high efficiency toward shared goals (Tuckman, 1965).

This framework offered a clear path for the team—which was stuck between storming and norming—to progress toward high-performing collaboration. My understanding of it became the foundation for designing a three-and-a-half-day retreat that would focus on building resilience through improved communication and emotional intelligence.

Retreat Agenda: Activities Designed for Connection and Growth

We began the retreat by establishing team touchstones, which served as the team's "rules of engagement"—a set of agreed-upon principles that would guide how they interacted, communicated, and supported one another throughout the retreat and beyond. These touchstones weren't just a list of aspirational behaviors; they were a shared commitment to creating a safe, collaborative, and respectful environment. They represented the collective promise of how the team would "show up" for each other during both smooth sailing and challenging times.

To break the ice and ease into the day, we used an activity called "All About Me." Each team member was invited to complete a large poster sheet, thoughtfully designed with four prompts: a date that held deep personal significance to them, a person who had profoundly influenced their life, something they felt deeply grateful for, and their personal hopes and aspirations for what they aimed to gain from the retreat. As participants shared their responses, walls began to come down. Vulnerability led to connection, and shared stories laid the groundwork for deeper conversations. Emotional intelligence was at play as team members practiced active listening and began to see each other as more than colleagues—they were individuals with unique journeys, strengths, and challenges.

Next, we lightened the mood with a "Guess Who" game, where team members brought baby and high school photos for the group to match with the person. This reminded the team that everyone had something in common, like a belly button. This playful activity wasn't just for fun; it helped the team relax, laugh together, and strengthen bonds in a non-threatening way. Moments of levity like these are critical in building resilient teams, as they remind everyone of the joy in connection and create a safe space for the harder conversations ahead.

The team playbook session became the heart of the retreat. Together, the team defined their values, behaviors, and superpowers—both as a group and as individuals. This collaborative effort provided clarity on how they could support one another, stay accountable, and leverage their collective strengths. The session also served as a reflection point, encouraging the team to acknowledge past missteps and commit to better communication moving forward. This exercise not only gave them practical tools but also reinforced the emotional intelligence skills of self-awareness, empathy, and adaptability—key ingredients for resilience in any team.

To deepen understanding, we explored the DiSC communication

styles inventory, an assessment that categorizes communication preferences into four styles: Dominance (D), Influence (I), Steadiness (S), and Conscientiousness (C). Through the assessment, each team member identified their unique communication preferences, D, I, S, C or a combination of the styles. By learning about their own styles and those of their colleagues, the team gained insights into potential friction points and strategies to adapt. This activity emphasized that communication isn't one-size-fits-all; instead, it requires intentionality and empathy. Resilient teams understand the value of meeting each other where they are, and this session provided the tools to do just that.

Emotional Intelligence in Action

One of the most transformative parts of the day was the "missing conversations" pods. In pairs, team members used a structured prompt—"I've been feeling less connected, and I want to reconnect"—to address unspoken tensions and build bridges. Each person had five uninterrupted minutes to share while their partner listened without judgment. This exercise fostered emotional safety and encouraged participants to lean into vulnerability, which is the bedrock of resilience. By confronting tensions constructively, the team turned potential conflict into meaningful connection.

To close the retreat, we introduced a reflective exercise called the six-word story. Each team member captured the essence of their retreat experience in just six words. These brief yet powerful stories highlighted the emotions, breakthroughs, and inspiration they had gained throughout the day. The exercise underscored how far

the team had come—not just in terms of practical outcomes but also in their ability to connect, support one another, and communicate effectively.

By creating space for personal connection, collaborative problem-solving, and honest communication, the retreat helped the team emerge stronger, more cohesive, and better equipped to navigate challenges together. Every element of it was designed to weave emotional intelligence and resilience into the fabric of the team's dynamics. It wasn't just a day of activities; it was a transformational experience that demonstrated the power of vulnerability and trust in building a resilient and high-performing team.

Turning Principles into Practice: The Retreat's Lasting Impact

The impact of the retreat became evident in the months that followed, as the team began to embody the principles and practices we had worked on together. At the six-month check-in, it was clear that the retreat had laid a strong foundation for change. Team members reported feeling more connected and supported. The team playbook wasn't just sitting on a shelf—it was actively referenced during meetings to ensure alignment with values and behaviors. Communication, a significant pain point before the retreat, had improved noticeably. People were more intentional about adapting their styles to others' preferences, a direct result of the DiSC inventory session. One team member even shared that they now felt comfortable addressing conflicts openly, which they had avoided in the past. The retreat's emphasis on creating a safe space for vulnerability had shifted the team culture in a profound way.

From Retreat to Resilience: A Year of Team Growth

By the one-year mark, the team had taken their progress even further. Trust had deepened, and they had collectively weathered significant challenges, including tight deadlines and shifting priorities, without the tension and miscommunication that previously held them back. They reported feeling more resilient as a unit, with a stronger ability to adapt to change and support one another. One standout example was how they used the "missing conversations" framework to address a misunderstanding before it escalated. Rather than letting issues fester, they proactively tackled the problem using the emotional intelligence skills they had honed during the retreat.

Perhaps the most telling sign of their growth was the feedback from new team members who joined during this time. They described the team as welcoming, clear about their values, and committed to collaboration. The "Guess Who" game had even become a fun tradition to integrate new hires, underscoring the importance of building personal connections. When asked to reflect on the team's journey, one senior member noted, "We're not just working together anymore; we're truly functioning as a team."

The progress at both six months and one year showed that the retreat wasn't a one-time event but a pivotal moment that reshaped the team's dynamics. The journey of this team demonstrates how deliberate efforts to foster emotional intelligence and resilience can lead to profound and lasting transformation. Their evolution from a group of individuals to a cohesive, collaborative unit highlights the transformative power of trust, communication, and shared purpose. But teamwork, much like nature, is not static—it ebbs and flows, thriving in some seasons and facing challenges in others.

To truly understand what it takes for teams to endure and grow, let's turn to a fitting analogy: the resilience of a forest through the ever-changing seasons.

Resilient Teams: Thriving Through the Four Seasons

Imagine your team as a forest—a living, breathing ecosystem where each member is a tree, rooted in shared values, weathering the ever-changing seasons of work life. But unlike trees, you all wear business casual instead of bark. (At least, I hope.) Resilient, emotionally intelligent teams don't just survive the seasons—they thrive through them, growing stronger, more connected, and occasionally laughing when someone trips over their own "roots."

Let's take a walk through this metaphorical forest, season by season, and explore how you can help your team flourish.

Spring: New Beginnings and Fresh Starts

Spring is the time of new projects, fresh ideas, and the occasional pollen allergy. In your team, this is when everyone is bursting with enthusiasm, brainstorming at lightning speed, and trying to figure out how to keep up with all those sticky notes.

What You Can Do:

- **Plant the seeds:** Encourage creative thinking and let every idea, even the bizarre ones, find some sunlight. (Yes, even Kim's idea about "Team Building Bowling.")

- **Water the roots:** Offer encouragement and support, especially to newer team members who might still be finding their footing.
- **Pull out weeds early**: Address potential issues before they grow into full-blown misunderstandings. Think of it as nipping drama in the bud—literally.

Spring is a season of optimism and opportunity, but it's also a time to gently guide your team toward alignment. After all, nobody wants a forest where half the trees are growing sideways.

Summer: Productivity in Full Bloom

Ah, summer—the season of long days, hard work, and someone always "forgetting" to turn on the AC. In your team, summer is when you're deep in the weeds of a big project, juggling deadlines, and occasionally pausing to swat at metaphorical mosquitoes (also known as last-minute client changes).

What You Can Do:

- **Keep your cool:** Practice emotional self-regulation to manage stress and remind everyone else to hydrate (literally and metaphorically).
- **Share your shade:** Be a team player. If someone's workload feels heavier than an oak tree, offer your help.
- **Celebrate the blooms:** Acknowledge progress and small victories. "Way to go, team!" goes a long way—even if the team is just trying to survive until happy hour.

Summer is the season of high energy and heavy workloads, but resilient teams know how to stay cool under pressure. Be the teammate who cranks up the metaphorical AC with humor and positivity.

Autumn: Change and Reflection

In autumn, the leaves start to fall, the air gets crisp, and everyone starts debating pumpkin spice lattes. For teams, this is a season of transition—a time to reflect on what worked, what didn't, and what needs to be raked up and tossed into the metaphorical compost pile.

What You Can Do:

- **Turn over a new leaf:** Encourage open discussions about how the team can improve. Be ready to admit, "Yeah, that one strategy was more of a dud than a pumpkin that didn't make it to Halloween."
- **Shed the dead weight:** Help your team let go of unproductive habits or outdated processes. Yes, even the spreadsheet no one understands but everyone is afraid to delete.
- **Plant seeds for the future:** Use lessons learned to prepare for the next big project. Don't forget to sprinkle in some optimism—it's fertilizer for team morale.

Autumn is the season for letting go—shake off what's holding your team back like trees dropping leaves, and gather up lessons like you're hoarding Halloween candy.

Winter: Weathering the Storms

Winter hits hard. Deadlines pile up like snowdrifts, resources are scarce, and tensions can run colder than your office thermostat. But like a forest enduring frost, resilient teams survive by sticking together, sharing resources, and knowing that spring is just around the corner.

What You Can Do:

- **Be the evergreens:** Provide stability and reliability during tough times. Be the person who says, "Let's figure this out together," even if you're quietly doing your own research to make it work.
- **Offer warmth:** Use empathy to check in on your teammates' emotional well-being. Sometimes, a simple "How are you holding up?" can melt the iciest tension.
- **Snowball fights, not cold shoulders:** Turn challenges into playful collaboration, not frosty avoidance. Bonus points if someone brings marshmallows for the cocoa.

Winter can feel like a never-ending grind, but resilient teams emerge stronger, like trees with frost-bitten branches that still find a way to grow new buds.

All-Season Tips for a Thriving Forest

No matter the season, some behaviors are always in style:

- **Listen to the wind:** Pay attention to subtle cues from your teammates, whether it's a sigh of frustration or a brilliant idea whispered in a brainstorming session.
- **Stay rooted:** Ground your team in shared values and a clear sense of purpose.
- **Bend, don't break:** Flexibility is the secret to surviving unexpected storms (or surprise audits).
- **Keep growing:** Foster a culture of continuous improvement, even if it's just learning how to make Monday meetings less painful.

Resilient teams, like forests, thrive because of their interconnected roots, their ability to adapt, and their shared strength. Whether your team is basking in the sunlight of summer or braving the chill of winter, the key is to embrace the season together—with humor, empathy, and a whole lot of resilience. After all, even the toughest storms can't stop a well-rooted team from growing stronger. As you reflect on the metaphor of a forest and its enduring resilience, consider how these principles apply to your own team dynamics. Building a resilient team requires more than just weathering the seasons; it calls for intentionality, self-awareness, and a commitment to growth.

The following reflection questions are designed to help you think deeply about your role in fostering emotional intelligence and resilience within your team. Use them as an opportunity to evaluate where you are, celebrate progress, and identify areas for continued growth. Just like a forest, the strength of your team lies in its roots—and in how each member contributes to the collective whole.

Reflection

Building Resilient Teams

Building a resilient team requires intentionality, self-awareness, and a shared commitment to growth. Just as the seasons bring different challenges and opportunities, teams evolve through cycles of change, progress, and adaptation. Resilient teams are those that embrace the seasons of their journey—budding with new ideas in spring, thriving under the heat of summer, shedding inefficiencies in autumn, and leaning on each other during the winter storms.

Grab some paper, choose a restful spot, and approach this reflection with honesty and care. The following reflection questions will guide you in thinking about your team's dynamics, evaluating strengths and opportunities for improvement, and taking actionable steps to foster emotional intelligence and resilience. Use this as an opportunity to dig into the "root system" of your team and identify ways to grow together through every season.

Think (Understanding & Awareness)

Consider these questions to explore your current understanding:

1. How would you describe your team's current "season" (spring, summer, autumn, or winter), and what does it reveal about your team's dynamics?
2. What do you believe are your team's core values? How do they guide your team's behavior and decision-making?
3. Reflect on a recent team success—what contributed to that moment, and how did the team collaborate to achieve it?
4. What role does trust play in your team's resilience, and how is it currently demonstrated or lacking?
5. How does your team handle stress or challenges during "winter" moments? Are there signs of isolation, or do members rally together?

Evaluate (Analyzing & Reflecting)

Take time to analyze and reflect on your emotional habits and patterns:

1. What are some "leaves" your team might need to shed—processes, behaviors, or habits that no longer serve the group's goals?
2. How does your team ensure all voices are heard during brainstorming or decision-making, especially during "spring" seasons of new ideas?

3. Reflect on a conflict your team has experienced. How was it resolved, and what lessons were learned about communication and collaboration?

4. How well does your team adapt to changing priorities or unexpected challenges, and what could improve this adaptability?

5. In what ways do team members currently demonstrate empathy and emotional intelligence toward one another?

Act (Implementation & Practice)

Turn your reflections into action with these practical steps:

1. What steps can you take to strengthen the "root system" of your team by building trust and fostering open communication?

2. How can you celebrate progress or small wins in your team to create a sense of achievement during busy "summer" periods?

3. What actions can you take to help your team reflect and adapt after a major project or transitional "autumn" phase?

4. How will you ensure emotional safety during moments of tension or conflict, encouraging "snowball fights" instead of "cold shoulders" in "winter?"

5. What's one specific behavior or mindset you will adopt to build resilience and emotional intelligence within your team starting today?

As you navigate the reflection questions, you've begun the journey of uncovering your team's dynamics and identifying opportunities for growth. But true resilience and emotional intelligence aren't built on introspection alone—they flourish through connection. To bring these concepts to life, we turn to a practical team-building activity: "All About Me." Designed to foster understanding, trust, and camaraderie, this exercise offers a creative and meaningful way to deepen bonds within your team. Let's shift from reflection to action, as you explore how shared stories can transform your team's vulnerability.

Team Activity

The "All About Me" Exercise

Team building often starts with breaking down barriers and creating an environment where individuals feel valued, seen, and understood. The "All About Me" Activity is a powerful way to set this tone, using personal storytelling to foster connection and empathy. This icebreaker goes beyond surface-level introductions, inviting team members to share meaningful insights about their lives. By creating space for vulnerability and active listening, this activity helps build emotional intelligence and resilience, laying the foundation for deeper collaboration and trust.

Through this exercise, team members begin to see each other not just as colleagues but as individuals with unique stories, values, and aspirations. Emotional intelligence comes into play as participants practice active listening, empathy, and open communication—essential skills for navigating the challenges of teamwork. Resilience grows as the team bonds over shared experiences, finding strength in their collective understanding and support.

How This Activity Builds Emotional Intelligence and Resilience

1. Fosters Empathy: By sharing personal moments, team members develop a deeper understanding of each other's journeys and perspectives.
2. Encourages Vulnerability: The prompts encourage participants to share authentic parts of themselves, building trust and a safe team environment.
3. Enhances Communication: Active listening during the sharing phase helps improve interpersonal communication skills.
4. Strengthens Team Dynamics: This activity creates a foundation for meaningful relationships, which are key to fostering a resilient and supportive team culture.

Facilitation Instructions

Materials Needed

- Large poster sheets or flip-chart paper (one per participant)
- Markers or pens in various colors
- Tape or sticky tack for displaying posters (optional)
- A timer (optional, for pacing the activity)
- A designated space for each participant to work on their poster

Preparation

1. Set the Space: Arrange a comfortable, informal setting where participants can work on their posters and share without distractions.

2. Prepare the Prompts: Write the four prompts on a whiteboard or share them verbally.

    - A date that holds deep personal significance to you.
    - A person who has profoundly influenced your life.
    - Something you feel deeply grateful for.
    - Your personal hopes and aspirations for what you aim to gain from this session or retreat.

3. Distribute Materials: Hand out a poster sheet and markers to each participant.

Step-by-Step Instructions

1. Introduce the Activity (5-10 minutes)

    - Explain the purpose of the activity and how it ties into the team's goals for emotional intelligence and resilience.
    - Emphasize that this is a safe space for sharing and that everyone's contributions are valued.

2. Create the Posters (20-30 minutes)

    - Ask each participant to divide their poster into four quadrants, dedicating one section to each prompt.
    - Encourage creativity—participants can write, draw, or use symbols to express their answers.

3. Sharing and Listening (5-10 minutes per participant)

    - Once everyone has completed their posters, invite participants to take turns presenting their quadrants to the group.
    - Encourage active listening during the presentations—remind

participants to be fully present and to avoid interrupting.
- After each presentation, allow a few minutes for the group to ask questions or share reflections (if comfortable).

4. Reflection and Discussion (15-20 minutes)

Facilitate a group discussion on the experience. Use guiding questions such as:

- "What did you learn about your teammates that surprised or inspired you?"
- "How does understanding someone's story change the way you view them as a colleague?"
- "How can the insights from this activity help us work better as a team?"

Tips for Success

- **Model Vulnerability:** As the facilitator, consider sharing your own responses to the prompts to set the tone and encourage openness.
- **Adapt for Time Constraints:** If time is limited, reduce the number of prompts or ask participants to share just one quadrant.
- **Create a Safe Space:** Remind everyone that participation is voluntary and that they can share as much or as little as they feel comfortable.

The "All About Me" activity is more than an icebreaker—it's a stepping stone toward building a resilient, emotionally intelligent team. By fostering empathy, strengthening connections, and encouraging open communication, this exercise helps team members cultivate the skills they need to navigate challenges and thrive together. Whether used to kick off a retreat or as a stand-alone team-building session, this activity can transform the way your team interacts and collaborates.

Ending for Chapter 10: Cultivating Resilient Teams

Building a resilient team is not a one-time effort—it's an ongoing journey of growth, adaptation, and connection. Through reflection, intentional practices, and activities like "All About Me," teams can strengthen their bonds, enhance their emotional intelligence, and create a culture of trust and collaboration. Much like a forest thriving through the changing seasons, resilient teams endure challenges, celebrate successes, and continuously nurture the roots that hold them together. They don't just weather storms—they grow stronger because of them. They embrace vulnerability, adapt to change, and prioritize connection over competition. As you consider the insights and tools shared in this chapter, reflect on how you can cultivate these qualities within your own team. The journey to resilience is not about perfection; it's about showing up with intention, empathy, and the courage to grow together.

With this foundation, your team is poised not only to achieve its goals but to thrive through every season, ready to face challenges with confidence and emerge stronger each time.

As we approach the conclusion of this book, take a moment to navigate to the chapter that resonates most with you right now, or continue on to the final chapter. In the closing, we will explore how to weave these lessons into the fabric of your journey and carry them forward into every aspect of your life.

Closing

- A PERSONAL NOTE OF GRATITUDE
- AN INVITATION TO CONTINUE THE JOURNEY
- FINAL REFLECTION: EXPLORING YOUR TAKE-AWAYS

Closing

As you turn the final page, I want to thank you—for your curiosity, your willingness to reflect, and your vulnerability in taking this journey with me. Writing this book has been an act of love, but it wouldn't have mattered without readers like you who are willing to put these principles into practice in their own lives.

It's a profound privilege to partner with you on this journey, even from afar. I know that opening yourself up to these ideas—digging deep into your own resilience and emotional intelligence—takes courage. I'm grateful that you trusted me enough to be part of that process.

Coaching is my passion, my calling, and my joy. Whether I'm working with an individual navigating their career, entrepreneur turning their vision into reality, a student stepping into their potential, a leader learning to guide with empathy, or a team striving to work better together, my mission is the same: To help people discover the strength, insight, and brilliance already within them—the best version of themselves. Every coaching session, retreat, and conversation is a reminder of the incredible capacity we all have to grow, connect, and make meaningful changes.

I hope you laughed, maybe cried a little, and most importantly, walked away with insights that feel actionable and authentic to your life. My goal wasn't to give you answers but to offer tools, stories, and reflections that spark your own path forward. I wanted to lead by example, sharing my own personal experiences—complete with the less-than-perfect moments—in the hope that it encourages you to keep pushing forward, no matter the setbacks. Every chapter draws inspiration from the incredible individuals and teams I've had the honor of coaching, whose courage to embrace vulnerability, strive for growth, and lead with authenticity has been nothing short of extraordinary.

Life is messy, beautiful, and endlessly unpredictable. But with emotional intelligence and resilience in your toolbox, you're ready to face it all. Keep growing, keep learning, and keep leaning into what makes you—and the world around you—stronger.

An Invitation to Continue the Journey

Know that the journey doesn't have to end here. If the stories, insights, and tools shared within these pages have sparked something in you—a question, a curiosity, or a desire to dig deeper—I would be honored to hear from you.

Whether you're an individual looking to navigate life's challenges with greater resilience, a leader striving to bring out the best in your team, or someone simply seeking to connect, I invite you to reach out.

Thank you for allowing me to be a part of your story. Here's to courage, growth, and the brilliance within you. Let's continue this conversation and make the world a little stronger—one connection at a time.

Warmly,

Coach Shirita Nash

Now, let's take a final moment to reflect on everything explored in this book.

Final Reflection

Exploring your Takeaways

Think (Understanding & Awareness)

Consider these questions to explore your current understanding:

1. What was your biggest takeaway about emotional intelligence from this book?
2. How do you currently define resilience in your own life?

3. Which story or metaphor in the book resonated most with your experiences? Why?
4. How have the chapter reflection questions helped you with self-awareness?

Evaluate (Analyzing & Reflecting)

Take time to analyze and reflect on your emotional habits and patterns:

1. Which chapter challenged you the most? Why?
2. How has your understanding of vulnerability changed throughout the book?

Act (Implementation & Practice)

Turn your reflections into action with these practical steps:

1. What is one specific action you'll take to strengthen emotional intelligence in your relationships?
2. How will you incorporate the principles of resilience into your daily routines or decision-making?
3. What's one way you can support a colleague, friend, or family member in building their resilience?
4. How will you hold yourself accountable for fostering trust and open communication in your teams?
5. What is one small change you can make today to embody the principles of emotional intelligence and resilience?

About the Author

Coach Shirita Nash is a distinguished leadership coach, program manager, and human resources expert with over 20 years of experience in shaping high-performing teams and fostering organizational excellence. Shirita is the founder of Acnestis Coaching & Consulting, LLC, a firm dedicated to helping individuals, teams, and organizations achieve their fullest potential. Acnestis offers a diverse range of services, including individual, executive, and team coaching, human resources consulting, workshops, behavioral assessments, and keynote speaking. Shirita's approach integrates data, behavioral science, and psychology with tailored strategies to foster growth and transformation.

Beyond her work at Acnestis, Shirita is the Agency Awards Program Lead at NASA. She manages the strategy and day-to-day operations of seven comprehensive awards and recognition programs, celebrating the extraordinary achievements of more than 18,000 civil servants and non-civil servants. Her exceptional contributions have earned her prestigious honors, including the Administrator's Exceptional Achievement Honor Medal and several Administrator's Agency Honor Awards.

Shirita's expertise extends across employee and labor relations, performance management, training and development, talent acquisition, change management, coaching, organizational development, and compliance in multiple organizations to include FedEx, BAE

Systems, and Enterprise Rent-A-Car. Through her leadership, Shirita has enhanced operational efficiencies, standardized processes, and cultivated a culture of innovation and appreciation within the private and public sector.

With a master's degree in human resources management from Nova Southeastern University and a bachelor's degree in psychology from the University of South Florida, Shirita brings a wealth of academic and professional expertise to her work. She holds numerous certifications, including ACC, ODCP, PMP, CPTD, SSGBC, SHRM-CP, and PHR, along with specialized proficiencies in executive and leadership development assessments. These credentials enable her to design personalized strategies that drive meaningful outcomes for her clients.

Through her writing and consulting, Shirita combines emotional intelligence and resilience with professional expertise to empower individuals and teams to thrive. Whether guiding leaders, executives, or entire organizations, she remains steadfast in her mission: to elevate humanity and well-being by helping others become the best versions of themselves.

Connect with Shirita Nash:

https://www.linkedin.com/in/shiritanash/

www.AcnestisCG.com

If this book resonates with you, I would love to hear your thoughts or feedback.

References

American Psychological Association. (2014). *The road to resilience*. Washington, DC: American Psychological Association. Retrieved November, 5, 2024, from https://www.apa.org/topics/resilience.

American Psychological Association. (n.d.). Social skills. In *APA Dictionary of Psychology*. Retrieved April, 14, 2024, from https://dictionary.apa.org/social-skills.

Angeleou, M. (2016, March 13). Maya Angelou's Post *Each one of us has lived through some devastation, some loneliness, some weather superstorm or spiritual superstorm, when we look*. Facebook. https://www.facebook.com/MayaAngelou/posts/10154284867709796/.

Anglund, J. W. (1967). *A cup of sun*. Harcourt, Brace & World.

Anne Lamott. (2015, April 8). *I am going to be 61 years old in 48 hours. Wow. I thought I was only forty-seven, but*. Facebook. https://www.facebook.com/AnneLamott/posts/662177577245222.

Bacal, J (Executive Producer). (1983–1986). G.I. Joe: A real American hero [Television series]. Sunbow Productions, Marvel Productions.

Bradberry, T., & Greaves, J. (2009). *Emotional intelligence 2.0*. TalentSmart.

Brown, B. (2018). *Dare to lead: Brave work. Tough conversations. Whole hearts.* Random House.

Brown, B. (2010, June). *The power of vulnerability* [Video]. TED Conferences. Retrieved from https://www.ted.com/talks/brene_brown_the_power_of_vulnerability.

The Dhammapada (T. Byrom, Trans.). (2006). Shambhala Publications. (Original work published ca. 3rd century BCE).

Dweck, C. S. (2006). *Mindset: The new psychology of success*. Random House.

Fredrickson, B. L. (2001). The role of positive emotions in positive psychology: The broaden-and-build theory of positive emotions. American Psychologist, 56(3), 218–226.

George Mason University. (n.d.). *Resilience model*. Retrieved February, 25, 2021, from https://wellbeing.gmu.edu/resources-2/resources/resilience-resources-weekly/#model.

Goleman, D. (1995). *Emotional intelligence: Why it can matter more than IQ*. Bantam Books.

Hanson, R. (2018). *Resilient: How to grow an unshakable core of calm, strength, and happiness*. Harmony Books.

Jordan, M. (1994). *I can't accept not trying: Michael Jordan on the pursuit of excellence*. HarperSanFrancisco.

Klemp, N., & Langshur, E. (2017). *Start here: Master the lifelong habit of wellbeing*. Simon & Schuster.

Mandela, N. (1994). *Long walk to freedom: The autobiography of Nelson Mandela*. Little, Brown and Company.

Maslow, A. H. (1943). A theory of human motivation. *Psychological Review*, 50(4), 370–396.

Nash, S. N., & Bricka, T. M. (2025). *Cracking the code: An integrated approach to meeting client needs at NASA's Langley Research Center.* Organization Development Review, 55(1), 17-23.

Pink, D. H. (2009). *Drive: The surprising truth about what motivates us*. Riverhead Books.

Seligman, M. E. P., & Csikszentmihalyi, M. (2000). Positive psychology: An introduction. American Psychologist, 55(1), 5–14.

Sinek, S. (2014). *Leaders eat last: Why some teams pull together and others don't*. Portfolio.

Tuckman, B. W. (1965). Developmental sequence in small groups. *Psychological Bulletin*, 63(6), 384–399.

Twain, M. (Attributed). The two most important days in your life are the day you are born and the day you find out why. (Source uncertain, commonly attributed to Mark Twain).

Wiseman, T. (1996). A concept analysis of empathy. *Journal of Advanced Nursing*, 23(6), 1162–1167.

Printed in Dunstable, United Kingdom

64853767R00167